THE QUICK AND SIMPLE 5-INGREDIENT LOW CHOLESTEROL COOKBOOK

LUNCIALEN GETIARRAZ

INTRODUCTION

Hello and welcome to "The Quick and Simple 5-Ingredient Low Cholesterol Cookbook". This book is more than a simple compilation of recipes; it is a beacon of hope for anyone grappling with high cholesterol levels and looking for a fresh start on the path to better health.

Many books focus on the 'what' and the 'how' of cooking - what ingredients to use, how to prepare them. This book indeed offers that, but it also endeavors to cover the 'why'. Why choose certain ingredients over others? Why maintain a low cholesterol diet? Why embrace cooking as an act of love and care for oneself and one's family? As we journey through the chapters, we will strive to address these whys, unraveling the mysteries and benefits of a low cholesterol diet.

Cholesterol is often demonized, but it's important to understand that not all cholesterol is bad. In fact, cholesterol is an essential component of every cell in our bodies, playing a vital role in various bodily functions. The problem arises when we have too much of a specific type, LDL or 'bad' cholesterol, which can contribute to atherosclerosis, potentially leading to heart disease. Thus, it becomes vital to balance our diet, to favor foods that help manage our cholesterol levels effectively.

This book aims to provide a bounty of culinary delights designed specifically to cater to individuals keen on reducing their cholesterol levels. Whether you're a novice in the kitchen or a seasoned home chef, these recipes will help make your cooking sessions a joy rather than a chore. We focus on simple, easy-to-source, and healthy ingredients that don't compromise flavor for the sake of nutritional value. Indeed, this cookbook's cornerstone is that health and taste can, and should, walk hand in hand.

Chapter One sets the stage, explaining why it is so crucial to manage cholesterol levels for overall better health. It will walk you through the fundamentals of cholesterol, the difference between 'good' and 'bad' cholesterol, and how diet plays a pivotal role in controlling and maintaining healthy cholesterol levels. The chapter will also guide you in making informed decisions about the foods you consume, and how simple tweaks in your diet can lead to significant changes in your cholesterol levels.

Breakfast is often said to be the most important meal of the day, and for good reason. It kick-starts our metabolism and provides the fuel we need to face the day ahead. Chapter Two offers a range of delectable breakfast recipes that are easy to prepare and are made with heart-healthy ingredients. From the refreshing Mango Tofu Smoothie to the hearty Savory Breakfast Rice Porridge, you'll find delicious options that set the right tone for your day.

Comfort food often takes the form of a warm, satisfying bowl of soup or stew, and Chapter Three acknowledges this. Here, you'll find recipes for hearty soups and stews that are not only nourishing but also packed with ingredients known for their cholesterol-lowering properties. Whether it's the hearty Bean and Quinoa Stew or the Tangy Fish and Tofu Soup, there's something for every palate.

Chapter Four takes us into the world of sandwiches, rolls, and wraps. These versatile and easy-to-prepare dishes are perfect for lunch, dinner, or anytime you need a quick, healthy bite. From Spicy Salmon Avocado Sandwich to Lean Beef Lettuce Wraps, each recipe combines taste and nutrition in a perfect harmony.

Chapter Five dives into the main courses, providing a wealth of recipes that would make the heart (quite literally) happy. It offers a range of dishes, from lean meats to vegetarian and vegan options, showcasing that a low-cholesterol diet does not have to be restrictive or monotonous.

Chapter Six offers an array of salads, sides, and snacks, each one simple, flavorful, and filled with heart-healthy ingredients. Whether it's the crunchy Cabbage and Carrot Salad, the fragrant Sesame Spinach, or the zesty Lemony Green Beans with Almonds, these recipes show that nutritious food can be as tantalizing to the palate as it is beneficial for your health.

Chapter Seven, a treasure trove of guilt-free desserts, is here to prove that a low-cholesterol diet doesn't mean bidding adieu to your sweet tooth. The recipes here, from Chocolate Chia Pudding to Honey-Garlic Sauce, prove that dessert can be healthy, satisfying, and delicious, all at the same time.

In the pursuit of health and wellness, many overlook the importance of flavor and enjoyment in their meals. This is a critical mistake, as savoring our food is not just a source of pleasure but also contributes to our overall sense of wellbeing. The dishes in this book have been thoughtfully designed to balance both health and taste, using only five main ingredients to keep things simple and accessible, even for those new to the kitchen.

Additionally, you'll notice that the ingredient lists are purposefully concise. This is not just to make the recipes easy and quick, but also to let each ingredient shine and contribute its unique flavor and health benefits. From heart-healthy fats like avocados and walnuts, fiber-rich ingredients like beans and lentils, to lean proteins like chicken and fish, every component has been chosen carefully to nourish your body while keeping cholesterol in check.

This book is your companion in health, guiding you to

cultivate habits of mindful eating. The act of preparing and consuming food can become a beautiful, fulfilling ritual, contributing significantly to your overall wellness journey. It is about changing your relationship with food, seeing it not just as sustenance, but as an opportunity to fuel your body with the nutrients it needs to thrive.

As you embark on this journey, remember that change doesn't occur overnight. It's about making small, consistent changes over time, and this applies to dietary changes as well. Start with a single recipe from this book, and gradually incorporate more over time. Soon, you'll find that your plate isn't just filled with low-cholesterol foods but a variety of flavors and colors that make each meal a delight.

In conclusion, "The Quick and Simple 5-Ingredient Low Cholesterol Cookbook" isn't just a cookbook; it's a guide, a friend, and a resource designed to help you navigate the path to healthier eating and living. Whether you're a seasoned chef or a novice cook, this book will inspire and equip you to make delicious, heart-healthy meals with ease and confidence. Happy cooking!

CONTENTS

Chapter One: Lower Your Cholesterol for Better Health
.... 1

Chapter Two: Breakfasts 2

Mango Tofu Smoothie 24

Blueberry Smoothie Bowl 25

Strawberry Yogurt Tarts... 26

Nut Butter Overnight Oats 28

Nutty Oat Bars 34

Blueberry Breakfast Muffins.. 36

Apple-Cinnamon Quinoa 38

Egg White, Parsley, and Pepper Cups 39

Savory Breakfast Rice Porridge.................................. 41

Chapter Three: Soups and Stews 49

Red Lentil Soup 50

Black Bean Soup 52

Butternut Squash Soup... 54

Hearty Bean and Quinoa Stew 56

Tangy Fish and Tofu Soup 58

Savory Chicken and Watermelon Rind Soup 60

Chicken and Rice Noodle Soup 62

Creamy Chicken and Corn Soup 64

Honey-Garlic Chicken Stew 66

Easy Turkey Chili 68

Lean Beef and Barley Soup 70

Chapter Four: Sandwiches, Rolls, and Wraps 76

Spicy Chickpea and Cilantro Wrap 79

Egg White and Avocado Breakfast Wrap 80

Spicy Salmon Avocado Sandwich 86

Chicken Pita Wraps with Oregano-Thyme Sauce 92

Chicken Pesto Baguette 94

Turkey Sloppy Joes 96

Lean Beef Lettuce Wraps 98

Chapter Five: Mains.. **101**

Spinach, Walnut, and Black Bean Burgers...................... 104

Loaded Veggie-Stuffed Peppers..................................... 106

Spicy Trout Sheet Pan Dinner 108

Maple-Garlic Salmon and Cauliflower Sheet Pan Dinner 110

Sweet Salad Dressing Chicken and Carrot Sheet Pan Dinner
.... 114

Chicken, Mushroom, and Bell Pepper Skewers 116

Chicken Curry 118

Lemon Chicken and Asparagus...................................... 120

Spicy Honey Chicken and Eggplant 122

Turkey Meatballs 124

Turkey Quinoa Casserole 126

Sheet Pan Honey-Soy Beef Broccoli 128

Heart-Healthy Meatloaf.. 130

Easy Lean Beef with Carrots and Potatoes 132

Chapter Six: Salads, Sides, and Snacks **136**

Cilantro-Lemon Quinoa Salad 139

Crunchy Cabbage and Carrot Salad............................... 142

Apple-Carrot-Kale Salad.. 143

Tomato Sauce–Simmered Eggplant............................. 145

Chili, Garlic, and Onion Kale Chips 147

Sesame Spinach... 149

Sweet Garlic-Vinegar Crushed Cucumber 151

Lemony Green Beans with Almonds 153

Chapter Seven: Desserts **157**

Chocolate Chia Pudding.. 158

Pumpkin Pie Pudding 162

Chocolate and Date Cupcakes..................................... 164

Blueberry Crumble... 166

Strawberry-Apple-Lemon Smoothie Pops 170

Apple-Cinnamon Flatbread.. 171

Apple-Honey Cupcakes 173

Honey-Garlic Sauce... 180

Sweet Salad Dressing 181

Tasty Tomato Sauce... 182

Spinach and Walnut Pesto 183

Tangy Soy Sauce 185

Oregano-Thyme Sauce 188

Measurement Conversions 190

Chapter One

Lower Your Cholesterol for Better Health

You might be reading this book because you or someone you care about just received a diagnosis of high cholesterol, or you might want to expand your diet after managing high cholesterol for some time. Either way, it's essential to understand how cholesterol affects your body. Knowing about the different types of cholesterol, how cholesterol affects health, and what factors increase cholesterol will clarify the role food plays in health. This book uses evidence-based eating guidelines to outline which foods help lower cholesterol. I'll also give you tips and tools to set your kitchen up for success. By the end, you'll see that eating a heart-healthy diet can be delicious, quick, and enjoyable.

Know Your Cholesterol

What is cholesterol, exactly? Cholesterol is a waxy substance in our blood that helps the body make hormones, assists with certain organ functions, and aids in the digestion of important nutrients and vitamins, including vitamin D. Cholesterol itself isn't inherently "unhealthy," but too much of it can lead to health problems.

Cholesterol comes from two sources. The first—blood cholesterol—is made by your body in your liver, and the second—dietary cholesterol—is found in foods (mainly animal products like meat, shellfish, dairy, and eggs). When a doctor says someone has high cholesterol, they are referring to the cholesterol levels that show up in blood tests, or blood cholesterol.

Although it's important to eat dietary cholesterol in moderation (especially if you have other health concerns, such as diabetes), it's blood cholesterol, specifically "lousy" low-density lipoprotein (LDL), that is the bigger health factor. According to the Harvard T. C. Chan School of Public Health, our blood cholesterol levels are influenced more by the fats we eat (namely trans fats and saturated fats) than by the amount of dietary cholesterol found in foods. Generally, foods that are high in saturated fats tend to be high in dietary cholesterol, too.

High saturated fat foods that increase the LDL cholesterol level include fatty meats, such as bacon, butter, palm/coconut oil, processed foods, and high-fat dairy, such as cheese. Trans fat foods include hydrogenated margarine and deep-fried foods. As a rule, try to limit saturated and trans fats foods to occasional treats. Unsaturated fats, which help maintain "healthy" high-density lipoprotein (HDL) cholesterol levels, include olive oil; nuts, such as almonds and walnuts; soft nonhydrogenated margarine; and fish, such as salmon. If you're unsure whether a fat is saturated or unsaturated, remember that saturated fats, such as butter, are usually solid at room temperature. Unsaturated fats, such as vegetable oil, tend to stay liquid.

TYPES OF CHOLESTEROL

As you just read, there are two types of blood cholesterol that impact your health: "healthy" HDL and "lousy" LDL.

Most of the cholesterol in the body is produced in a healthy liver. HDL is considered healthy because it helps move excess cholesterol out of your blood to the liver, where it is broken down and removed from the body. LDL is considered lousy because it plays a role in cholesterol build-up inside the blood vessels that can cause blockages and lead to heart disease, heart attacks, and strokes.

This cookbook offers recipes that help lower LDL levels and maintain healthy HDL levels. They do this by using ingredients that are low in dietary cholesterol, low in saturated fats, low in trans fats, low in sodium, high in fiber, and have healthy amounts of unsaturated fats.

HOW CHOLESTEROL AFFECTS YOUR HEALTH

Imagine blood vessels are like streets, and the blood that carries nutrients or oxygen to all the body's parts are the cars. No litter or other obstructions (good blood flow) allows the blood to reach our organs efficiently. LDL cholesterol is like litter that slowly builds up over time and can create blockages that prevent the cars (our blood) from driving smoothly through the streets (blood vessels). HDL cholesterol is like a garbage truck that helps carry cholesterol back to the liver, where it is broken down. As I mentioned previously, diets that are high in saturated fats, high in trans fats, and low in unsaturated fats can increase LDL cholesterol (the litter blocking the traffic).

When LDL cholesterol is high, plaque or blockages in the blood vessels can form, which causes the arteries to narrow or harden. These blockages and hardened arteries increase the risk of heart disease, high blood pressure, heart attacks, and strokes. These are a few reasons why we need to maintain healthy cholesterol levels.

Eating less bacon and butter, minimizing salt intake, and eating more fiber can help lower cholesterol and maintain good heart health. It might feel like a big challenge at first to make these types of dietary changes. I understand that. When changing your eating patterns, it can help to start with small, manageable alterations and work your way up. Try choosing 1 to 2 recipes from this book to begin, then slowly increase the number of recipes you try every week.

Know the Signs

High cholesterol can lead to several detrimental health effects, including high blood pressure, heart attack, or stroke. High blood pressure is when the force of blood against the blood vessel walls is high, and your heart needs to work harder than usual to pump blood. A heart attack is when the flow of blood to the heart is blocked, causing damage. A stroke is when the blood flow to the brain is blocked, which causes cells of the brain to die. Knowing the signs for each of these issues can save a life. If you're experiencing any of these symptoms, or if you see someone experiencing these symptoms, seek immediate medical attention.

Signs of a heart attack include chest pain or discomfort that might spread to your upper back, neck, or jaw.

Signs of a stroke include numbness on one side of the body, confusion, headache, dizziness, vision change, or trouble speaking.

Lowering Cholesterol Through Diet

Lowering your cholesterol with a heart-healthy diet is easier with the right tools in place, including knowing the daily limits for unhealthy fats, how to choose better-for-you foods, how to read labels, and how to prep your kitchen. Although any change is difficult at first, following these guidelines is a breeze once you get the hang of them. And I'm here to show you how. This book makes lowering your cholesterol more manageable by taking out the guesswork. The recipes are all low in saturated fat, trans fat, dietary cholesterol, and sodium while being rich in dietary fiber and unsaturated fats.

EATING GUIDELINES TO LOWER CHOLESTEROL

The American Heart Association (AHA) recommends a heart-healthy diet to improve cholesterol levels. This entails:

Limiting saturated and trans fats. In healthy adults, that means limiting your saturated fat intake to 10 percent of the total calories you eat per day. For example, an adult with healthy cholesterol levels consuming 2,000 calories a day should aim for 22 grams or less of saturated fat. People with a high LDL cholesterol level with an increased risk for heart disease should eat less saturated fat—6 to 7 percent of total calories. On a 2,000-calorie-a-day diet, that means no more than 120 calories, or 13 grams, should come from saturated fat.

Eating unsaturated fats. The AHA also recommends replacing saturated fats with unsaturated fats; for example, swapping butter with olive oil and avoiding foods containing trans fat. There is no upper limit on unsaturated fats per day, but fats, even healthy, unsaturated ones, are high in calories, so should be enjoyed in moderation. The AHA offers general guidelines to lower your cholesterol, but always check with your doctor or health care practitioner for your individual health needs and limits.

Limiting dietary cholesterol. In addition to monitoring the types of fat, the AHA, the US Department of Agriculture, and the American College of Cardiology all suggest reducing dietary cholesterol in your diet, although specific recommendations were not given. Thankfully, that is easy to do because diets that are low in saturated fats and trans fats tend to be low in dietary cholesterol, too.

Reducing sodium. The AHA suggests limiting sodium to 2,300 milligrams (around 1 teaspoon of salt) a day to improve heart health and lower cholesterol. Sometimes, depending on your health care provider's recommendations and your particular needs, the sodium recommendation is even less (1,500 milligrams).

Increasing fiber. Consuming fiber is another excellent way to lower cholesterol and reduce the risk of heart disease. The FDA suggests at least 25 grams of fiber daily on a 2,000-calorie diet. Some good sources of fiber include whole grains, fruits, vegetables, legumes, nuts, and seeds.

If you don't have the energy to determine how much fat, sodium, and fiber is in every food you eat, don't worry. This book will make adhering to these guidelines easy. Just glance at the nutrition bar at the bottom of each recipe to see the amounts of saturated and unsaturated fats, fiber, sodium, and more to keep your health goals on track.

Risk Factors

There are two types of risk factors to consider when looking at cholesterol and heart disease— controllable and noncontrollable.

Controllable risk factors are choices you can make, such as exercising, eating a healthy diet, getting adequate sleep, managing stress levels, drinking less alcohol, and not smoking. You can reduce controllable risk factors with simple lifestyle changes. For example, take a 15-minute walk three times a week for one month or make a lovely nutritious dinner at home instead of ordering out. When you make those home-cooked meals, choose fish at least twice a week instead of red meat. Another way to change your habits is to make a list of your current routines, such as your exercise program, diet, sleep schedule, etc., and then brainstorm healthier lifestyle changes. You can write your ideas down in a journal and attach achievable timelines to your new goals. Be sure to celebrate your achievements.

Noncontrollable risk factors involve genetics or family history, including age (heart-health issues tend to increase as we get older) and sex (incidences develop earlier in men than in women).

Although you can't change your genetic makeup or your age, you *can* make many lifestyle changes to lower your cholesterol, and the recipes in this book will empower you to do just that.

CHOOSING FOODS TO LOWER CHOLESTEROL

Choosing heart-healthy foods helps maintain the healthy HDL cholesterol levels and decrease the lousy LDL levels. What are some of these heart-healthy foods and how often should you eat them? Let's dive into some specifics.

Fats. Good sources of unsaturated fats include fish, such as salmon, trout, and tuna. Choose fresh or frozen fish and low-sodium canned versions. Avoid deep-fried fish. Try to enjoy fish twice weekly, as a main dish at dinner or for lunch in a sandwich or wrap. Other sources of unsaturated fats include vegetable oils, such as olive oil, as well as nuts, seeds, and soy products. Use olive oil instead of butter when cooking or baking. Keep in mind that coconut oil and palm oil are higher in saturated fat and should be limited. Have nuts and seeds as a snack or add them as toppings to yogurt, oatmeal, or homemade baked goods. Tofu can increase the healthy fats and protein in your diet, so add it to soups and other dishes. Finally, trans fats are often found in deep-fried foods, such as French fries, donuts, battered foods, and chips, and these foods should be limited.

Fiber. Choosing to eat dietary fiber often helps lower the LDL level in the body. Sources of dietary fiber include vegetables, fruits, whole grains, legumes, nuts, and seeds. Try adding more fresh, frozen, or dried fruit or vegetables to your daily plate. Whole grains such as oatmeal, barley, and multigrain bread are excellent sources of fiber. Try legumes like lentils, beans, and chickpeas in soups, salads, or wraps, and throw a little nut butter in your baking. Remember, increase your fiber intake gradually and drink plenty of water daily to help with digestion.

Meat and dairy. High saturated fat animal products include butter; full-fat milk products, such as heavy cream and cheeses; fatty cuts of meat; and processed meats, such as bologna or hot dogs. Replace these items with low-fat dairy products and choose leaner cuts of meat at the market. Leaner meats include round; chuck; sirloin or loin (in beef); tenderloin or loin chop (in pork); or the leg, arm, and loin (in lamb). When eating poultry, remove the skin and discard it.

Sodium. Reducing sodium can help decrease the risk of heart disease. High quantities of sodium are often found in restaurant dishes or takeout foods, processed meats, premade frozen foods, and some canned foods. Be sure to check nutrition labels and limit food products with higher sodium levels.

THE 5-INGREDIENT PROMISE

One way you can avoid saturated fat, trans fats, and sodium is to limit the number of ingredients in recipes. Fewer ingredients means less chance of adding ones that are unhealthy. This book promises recipes that are 5 ingredients or fewer, minus the "freebie" staples of water, oil, salt, and pepper.

Recipes with lots of ingredients mean more shopping trips and longer prep times, which is what you don't need after a long day of work, school, or other obligations. As a registered dietitian and coach, I know firsthand the challenges people face when transitioning to a healthier lifestyle, and I want to simplify it for you.

Recipes with limited ingredients help you or a loved one achieve the goals of lowering cholesterol through a heart-healthy diet. Fewer ingredients means less chopping, seasoning, and active preparation times. And as a bonus, these recipes are also easier on the wallet because you'll be buying fewer groceries.

Life is full of challenges. Eating well should not be one of them. The 5-ingredient promise makes eating healthy to lower cholesterol not only easy, but tasty. Using fresh and whole foods helps reduce the time and energy it takes to get a dish from the page to the table without sacrificing flavor and nutrition.

Check in with Your Doctor or Health Care Provider

This book aims to provide a general guideline for people who want to lower their cholesterol through heart-healthy eating. However, each person has unique health issues, needs, and physiologies. As previously mentioned, there are risk factors you can't control, such as genetics or family history, age, and sex. With these factors in mind, it is best to check in with your doctor or health care provider to get their specific recommendations for your individual health guidelines.

Your doctor may also prescribe medications to help lower your cholesterol or ask you to make dietary changes, limit your consumption of alcohol, quit smoking, or increase your level of exercise. Ask your doctor for more information about community support groups to help, and how often you should be getting regular checkups. Good communication with your health care team is essential for good health.

Cooking in Your Low-Cholesterol Kitchen

A well-stocked kitchen makes it easier to cook, eat, and live a heart-healthy lifestyle. The first thing to consider is your pantry and refrigerator, starting with the building blocks of these recipes—the ingredients.

MOVE THESE OUT

First, you'll want to remove (or cut way back on) foods that are high in saturated fat, trans fat, and sodium. Refer to the chart here for a handy cheat sheet, or read on for more detailed information.

HIGH SATURATED FAT	HIGH TRANS FAT
• Butter, lard • Coconut oil, palm oil • Deli or processed meats, such as sausage, salami, bologna, and hot dogs • Fatty meats, such as bacon, heavily marbled steak, ribs, and ground beef • Full-fat milk, cheeses, ice cream • Heavy cream, full-fat yogurt, sour cream • Pâté • Skin-on poultry, chicken wings • Store-bought muffins, croissants, bread, strudels,	• Breaded, battered, fried foods • Chips • Donuts • French fries, onion rings • Hydrogenated margarine • Instant noodles **HIGH SODIUM**

cakes, pies, donuts, cookies	• Bouillon cubes • Canned foods • Frozen, ready-made meals • Pre-made gravies, sauces

Saturated fats are mostly found in animal products such as deli meats, sausages, and bacon. Fattier meats include heavily marbled meats, ribs, or regular ground beef. Skin-on poultry is a higher source of saturated fats, as are spreads such as pâté, made from the liver and other animal parts. Coconut and palm oil come from plants and, as such, are "sneaky" forms of saturated fats. Coconut and palm oils are readily available and fairly inexpensive to produce, so they are found in many processed or ready-made products. Other foods to avoid include store-bought baked goods, which often contain hidden sources of saturated fats.

Trans fats are found in hydrogenated margarine and deep-fried foods. The process of hydrogenation in certain margarines creates trans fats as a side product. Instant ramen noodles can be a hidden source of trans fat, so check the label. Other potential sources of trans fats include chips, French fries, onions rings, donuts, and breaded or battered foods deep fried in oil.

Sodium is often added to foods to preserve their shelf life or for fermentation. It can be found in premade gravies, sauces, ready-made meals, certain canned foods, and bouillon cubes.

MOVE THESE IN

The following heart-healthy ingredients are used in this book's recipes and may help you lower your cholesterol. They include good sources of unsaturated fats and dietary fiber, or are low in saturated fats, trans fats, dietary cholesterol, and sodium. The chart here organizes the ingredients into pantry, refrigerator, or freezer.

In the pantry, keep plenty of dried fruit, unsalted nuts, and seeds available for healthy snacks, salad toppings, or healthy homemade baked goods. Cooking oil, such as olive oil, is used in most of the recipes in this book. Individual spices or spice mixes without salt are an excellent way to add plenty of flavor to your meals. Steel-cut oats; quinoa; barley; brown rice; and whole-grain breads, crackers, pasta, and pitas are high in dietary fiber. Low-sodium sauces and low-sodium canned beans, lentils, fish, and certain vegetables are convenient and cut prep time. Nut butter and homemade popcorn are great choices for healthy snacks.

The freezer is a lifesaver when preparing meals for busy weeks. Lean meats, fish, and skinless chicken or turkey are freezer staples for healthy weeknight dinners. Frozen fruits are fantastic for smoothies or healthy baking, and frozen vegetables make a quick and healthy side dish. Low-fat ice cream or frozen yogurt can be a creamy treat at the end of your meal.

The refrigerator should contain a good rotation of seasonal fruits and vegetables for snacks and meals. Pre-minced herbs and aromatics, such as garlic or ginger, make prep time faster. Proteins such as low-fat yogurt, cheeses, and milks; lean meats; tofu; fish; skinless chicken and turkey; and eggs or egg whites are other staples. Nonhydrogenated margarines are an acceptable butter replacement since they are low in trans fats. Last, ingredients such as low-sodium soy sauce, vinegar, or low-sodium tomato sauce, are excellent for basic sauces and salad dressing recipes.

PANTRY	FREEZER
• Brown rice	• Fish, such as salmon
• Dried fruit	• Frozen fruits and vegetables
• Individual spices	• Lean meats
• Low-sodium canned fish	• Low-fat ice cream or frozen yogurt
• Low-sodium canned or dried legumes	• Skinless chicken and turkey
• Low-sodium canned vegetables	

PANTRY	REFRIGERATOR
• Low-sodium soy sauce	
• Nut butters	• Eggs and egg whites
• Popcorn kernels	• Fish, such as salmon
• Quinoa or barley	• Fresh fruits and vegetables
• Seeds, such as chia or sunflower seeds	• Lean meats, or meat alternatives like tofu
• Steel-cut oats	• Low-fat yogurts, cheeses, milks, or fortified milk alternatives
• Unsalted nuts, such as almonds	• Nonhydrogenated margarine
• Vegetable oil, such as olive or canola oil	• Pre-minced seasoning, such as garlic or ginger
• Vinegar	• Skinless chicken and turkey
• Whole-grain breads	
• Whole-grain crackers	
• Whole-grain pita	
• Whole-grain pasta	

Reading Labels

Knowing what to look for on nutrition labels helps you make smarter decisions about your cholesterol health. Here's a refresher if you need it.

All the information in the nutrition table is based on the serving size. If the serving size is ½ cup and you consume 1 cup of the food, then you need to double the values in the nutrition table. After the serving size, look at the calories and the percent daily value (%DV). The percent daily value is meant as a guide to the nutrients in a single serving of food.

Nutrients to consume more often include fiber, vitamin D, iron, and calcium, and nutrients to limit are saturated fat, trans fat, sodium, and cholesterol. Remember that if you're looking to lower your cholesterol level and improve your heart health, you want to aim for less than 13 grams of saturated fats and 2,300 mg of sodium daily. When looking at the ingredient section of a label, keep in mind the ingredients are listed by weight—the ingredient that weighs the most is first; the one that weighs the least is last.

If a food product claims to have "more," "fortified," or "enriched" ingredients or nutrients, it means the product has increased amounts of this nutrient. If it says "free," "low," or "reduced," there are decreased amounts of the nutrient.

The Tools You Will Use

Now that we've revamped the pantry, refrigerator, and freezer, we will look at the equipment, tools, and utensils used to make the delicious, healthy meals in this book. You may have most of these items already.

UTENSILS AND EQUIPMENT

○ **Baking dish (9-by-13-inch):** A baking or casserole dish is a deep, large pan used to cook or bake in the oven or as a serving dish. Choose one that is sturdy. Bonus points if it comes with a lid for easy storing.

○ **Baking sheets:** These are perfect for baking vegetables, meats, and other goodies in the oven. Preparing sheet pan dinners on weeknights can make for easy and efficient meals.

- **Blender:** You'll use a blender to pulse, puree, and liquefy smoothies, sauces, dips, soups, and desserts.
- **Can opener:** Look for one that is resistant to rust, dishwasher-safe, and sturdy. I use a can opener designed for both left- and right-handed people.
- **Colander:** Colanders are useful for draining pasta, meats, vegetables, and beans.
- **Cutting board:** Wooden or plastic cutting boards are both excellent options. Choose the cutting board that best suits your kitchen needs. Wooden cutting boards tend to be durable and less slippery, and plastic cutting boards are easier to wash, so they are suitable for raw meats.
- **Food thermometer:** It will let you know when you have achieved the minimum internal temperature for food safety.
- **Grater:** Choose a four-sided box grater that is easy to use. Graters are used for grating chocolate or cheese, zesting fruit, slicing vegetables, and more.
- **Knife sharpener:** Keep your knives sharp and ready for anything you throw at them.
- **Knives:** You'll need a chef's knife, a paring knife, and a serrated knife. A chef's knife is multipurpose and usually between 6 and 10 inches long. A paring knife is shorter, and used for slicing and trimming. A serrated knife is excellent for tomatoes, bread, and foods with a different texture on the outside than the inside.
- **Ladle:** Use a ladle for serving soups, stews, sauces, and drinks.
- **Large stockpot:** This is great for stews, soups, pasta, and sauces.
- **Measuring cups:** Look for measuring cups with clear measurement labeling. Get a set of dry cups and wet cups in 1-, ½-, ¾-, and ¼-cup measures.
- **Measuring spoons:** Buy a stackable set of measuring spoons that measure 1 tablespoon, ½ tablespoon, 1

teaspoon, ½ teaspoon, ¼ teaspoon, and ⅛ teaspoon.

- **Mixing bowls:** Get two large mixing bowls and one medium mixing bowl in stainless steel, if possible. Mixing bowls are used for everything from batters to marinades to sauces.
- **Muffin pans:** These pans are great for savory breakfast cups, desserts, and, of course, muffins.
- **Oven mitts:** Look for a comfortable, durable, washable material that can withstand high heat.
- **Skillet:** A skillet has a wide flat bottom and high, straight sides. It is used for sautéing, poaching, braising, simmering, and more.
- **Storage containers:** Prepping meals ahead of time and storing leftovers is an essential time-saver. Choose containers in various sizes that are safe to use in the dishwasher, microwave, refrigerator, and freezer.
- **Tongs:** Tongs have multiple purposes, from flipping food to serving pasta or salads. Look for tongs with a handy silicone grip so that they are easier to hold and provide some heat protection.
- **Vegetable peeler:** Choose a durable and sharp peeler, either straight or Y-shaped. You'll need it for peeling fruits and vegetables, as well as for shaving cheese and chocolate.

SPLURGE-WORTHY ITEMS

While not essential items, these splurge-worthy tools can make preparation, cooking, and cleaning easier and more efficient.

Cast-iron Dutch oven: What *can't* a cast-iron Dutch oven do? They are durable and last for years—sometimes for generations—and have been passed down in the family. This tool browns, boils, braises, and bakes a variety of meats, vegetables, stews, and more. A Dutch oven transitions from the stovetop to oven easily, so you can use it as a slow

16

cooker, casserole, or bread pan, which means less cleanup. Lastly, some are enormous, so you can make larger meals to portion and store for a later date.

Electric pressure cooker, such as an Instant Pot: These devices are energy-efficient, heat up quickly, and require less liquid than other cooking methods. Electric pressure cookers can cook just about anything—and fast. All the delicious juices stay right in your food, which means that not only is your food moist, but the water-soluble vitamins are retained rather than leached out. Like a Dutch oven, pressure cookers serve multiple purposes, from braising to baking to making rice, yogurts, and even cheesecakes. It can also be used for sterilization since water boils in it at high temperatures.

Food processor: Food processors are fantastic for decreasing prep time because they make chopping, slicing, pureeing, and shredding a breeze. Some food processors can knead dough and juice fruits and vegetables as well. A food processor makes preparing meals, from soups to salads to pasta dishes to baked goods, more efficient.

High-quality knives: High-quality knives are made with better steel, so sharpening the blade is easier, and the edge lasts longer. I use my knives every day, so splurging on higher quality was the way to go. Better knives also have more comfortable handles, which make them more user friendly. Generally, the weight and comfort of a good knife are benefits for the chef.

Stainless steel cookware: This cookware is easy to clean and low-maintenance because it is dishwasher safe. Stainless steel is also durable, unlike other cookware that may chip, stain, or rust. It heats quickly and uniformly, allowing faster, more efficient cooking times. Also, stainless steel does not create any chemical reaction with ingredients, so it does not affect the food's true flavors.

Clockwise from top left: <u>Spinach and Walnut Pesto</u>; <u>Honey-Garlic Sauce</u>; <u>Spicy Honey Sauce</u>; <u>Tangy Soy Sauce</u>

About the Recipes

Eating heart-healthy can be challenging, but making meals with just a few ingredients simplifies things. Each of the following delicious, nutritious recipes uses 5 ingredients or fewer, excluding salt, pepper, oil, and water. I have also included labels that specify preparation details, and there is a nutrition bar at the end of each recipe.

The prep labels include 30-Minute, One Pot, and No Cook. The 30-Minute label means the dish takes 30 minutes or less to make, including prep and cook times. The One Pot label means the dish is prepared in one cooking vessel to make cleanup easier. The No Cook label means there is no cooking necessary. These labels offer you another quick and easy reference point to determine if a recipe will work in your schedule.

The nutrition bar will help you keep track of nutrients related to your health, including ones important for lowering cholesterol, such as calories, total fat, saturated fat, trans fat, protein, carbohydrates, fiber, sodium, and potassium.

Let's get cooking!

Blueberry Smoothie Bowl

Chapter Two

Breakfasts

Mango Tofu Smoothie
Blueberry Smoothie Bowl
Strawberry Yogurt Tarts
Nut Butter Overnight Oats
Banana Oat Pancakes
Raisin Breakfast Cookies
Nutty Oat Bars
Blueberry Breakfast Muffins
Apple-Cinnamon Quinoa
Egg White, Parsley, and Pepper Cups
Savory Breakfast Rice Porridge
Oven-Baked French Toast
Spinach, Mushroom, and Egg White Omelet

Mango Tofu Smoothie

30-MINUTE, NO COOK

SERVES 3 • PREP TIME: 5 minutes

Smoothies are a perfect breakfast for those days when you need to eat on the go or are traveling early in the morning. If you enjoy a thicker smoothie, add more fruit or tofu. If you enjoy a thinner texture, add more liquid. My kids grew up with the taste and texture of tofu, so this recipe needed no hard sell in our household. However, if you are new to tofu, you may want more fruit to get to the desired texture.

---

1 banana
1 cup mango, fresh or frozen
¾ cup soft tofu
½ cup orange juice
½ cup low-fat milk

In a blender, place the banana, mango, soft tofu, orange juice, and milk and blend until smooth, about 30 seconds to 1 minute. Serve immediately.

Cooking tip: Divide the smoothie mixture into three Popsicle molds and freeze for a wonderful summertime treat.

PER SERVING (1 CUP): Calories: 143; Total fat: 3g; Saturated fat: 1g; Trans fat: 0g; Protein: 7g; Total carbohydrate: 25g; Fiber: 2g; Sodium: 25mg; Potassium: 442mg

Blueberry Smoothie Bowl

30-MINUTE, NO COOK

MAKES 2 • PREP TIME: 10 minutes

Smoothie bowls are another speedy and colorful breakfast to enjoy on a busy morning. Eating a smoothie in a bowl with a spoon rather than drinking it makes it seem more like a luxurious treat. This dish is kid-friendly, too. On Sunday mornings, my daughter often asks to help me make breakfast. She has loads of fun throwing all the ingredients into the blender, and she thinks it's a special treat when she picks her own toppings.

1 cup fresh berries (such as strawberries, blueberries, or blackberries), plus more for topping
1 banana
½ cup low-fat plain Greek yogurt
½ cup low-fat milk
1 tablespoon crushed almonds

1. In a blender, place the berries, banana, yogurt, and milk and blend until smooth.
2. Pour the smoothie into a bowl and top with crushed almonds and fresh berries.

Variation tip: Go wild with the toppings! Try adding other fruits, nuts, or seeds, such as chia seeds, and dried fruits such as pineapple.

PER SERVING (1 CUP): Calories: 140; Total fat: 2g; Saturated fat: 0g; Trans fat: 0g; Protein: 6g; Total carbohydrate: 26g; Fiber: 4g; Sodium: 56mg; Potassium: 420mg

Strawberry Yogurt Tarts

NO COOK

MAKES 5 • PREP TIME: 15 minutes, plus 2 hours to set

These frozen yogurt tarts are so decadent, it is like having dessert for breakfast. I often enjoy these cool treats on the patio on sweltering summer mornings after family sleepovers. Add additional crushed nuts or fresh fruit to the top of the yogurt before freezing for an extra heart-healthy boost, not to mention a bonus pop of flavor and texture.

½ **cup pitted Medjool dates**
½ **cup crushed almonds**
1 **tablespoon maple syrup**
1 **cup low-fat plain Greek yogurt**
½ **cup strawberries**
2 **tablespoons water**

1. Line 5 cups of a muffin tin with paper liners and set aside.
2. In a food processor or blender, place the dates and pulse for 10 to 20 seconds until they become a paste.
3. Add the crushed almonds and maple syrup to the blender and pulse to mix.
4. Evenly divide the date mixture into the lined cups and press it down firmly; it should fill about one-third of the cup.
5. In a clean blender, blend the yogurt, strawberries, and water until smooth.
6. Pour the fruit and yogurt mixture into the cups until each one is full.
7. Place the cups in the freezer for 2 hours to set, and serve.

Variation tip: Add 1 teaspoon of lime juice to the fruit and yogurt mixture for a tangy variation.

PER SERVING (1 TART): Calories: 141; Total fat: 5g; Saturated fat: 1g; Trans fat: 0g; Protein: 5g; Total carbohydrate: 20g; Fiber: 3g; Sodium: 35mg; Potassium: 310mg

Nut Butter Overnight Oats

NO COOK

SERVES 1 • PREP TIME: 5 minutes, plus 3 hours to chill

Oats are an excellent source of fiber and a great way to lower cholesterol at the start of the day. These overnight oats are also easy to make in batches on the weekend for the busy week ahead. If you make this recipe in a portable glass jar (like a Mason jar), it can be a great on-the-go meal. If nuts don't excite you or you have an allergy, substitute pureed fruit, such as berries or mangoes, for the nut butter. Some people enjoy eating these oats cold, but I prefer to warm them up in the microwave for 30 seconds.

¾ **cup low-fat milk**
½ **cup steel-cut oats**
2 **tablespoons nut butter (such as almond, cashew, or all-natural peanut butter)**
1 **tablespoon chia seeds**
1 **teaspoon maple syrup**

1. In a resealable container, mix the milk, oats, nut butter, chia seeds, and maple syrup.
2. Seal the container and place it in the refrigerator for three hours or overnight. Enjoy warm or cold.

Ingredient tip: If you use a plant-based milk alternative, make sure it is fortified with calcium and vitamin D, which are excellent nutrients for bone health.

PER SERVING (1 CUP): Calories: 680; Total fat: 28g; Saturated fat: 5g; Trans fat: 0g; Protein: 25g; Total carbohydrate: 88g; Fiber: 16g; Sodium:

86mg; Potassium: 920mg

Banana Oat Pancakes

30-MINUTE

MAKES 7 PANCAKES • **PREP TIME:** 5 minutes • **COOK TIME:** 20 minutes

Do you have an overripe banana sitting on your counter? These oat pancakes are an excellent way to use up this fruit because the banana's sweetness brings out the deep honey flavors in the oats. Bananas are also an excellent source of vitamin B_6, fiber, and potassium. So, treat yourself to a relaxing morning at home with these fluffy pancakes.

1 cup steel-cut oats
1 banana
1 large egg
½ cup low-fat milk (or plant-based alternative)
2 teaspoons baking powder
Olive oil

1. In a blender, place the oats, banana, egg, milk, and baking powder and blend until smooth, about 20 seconds.
2. Place a medium skillet over medium heat and coat it with olive oil.
3. Using ¼-cup measurements, add the batter to the hot skillet to form 4 pancakes.
4. Cook the pancakes until the edges turn slightly golden, about 2 minutes. Then flip them and cook for another 2 minutes on the other side. Remove the pancakes from the skillet and repeat with the remaining batter. Serve immediately.

Variation tip: Add 2 teaspoons of cocoa powder (to make chocolate pancakes) or 2 teaspoons of matcha green tea powder (for a change in flavor).

Storage tip : Store the cooled pancakes in an airtight container for up to 5 days in the refrigerator.

PER SERVING (1 PANCAKE): Calories: 143; Total fat: 3g; Saturated fat: 1g; Trans fat: 0g; Protein: 5g; Total carbohydrate: 23g; Fiber: 3g; Sodium: 19mg; Potassium: 336mg

Raisin Breakfast Cookies

30-MINUTE

MAKES 16 COOKIES • **PREP TIME:** 10 minutes • **COOK TIME:** 20 minutes

A batch of these cookies gets eaten very quickly in my household—because they're heart-healthy, but still feel indulgent. They are great for breakfast, snack time, or even after dinner. They are easily packed for travel and, because of their smaller size, the portions are ideal for children. My 3-year-old loves these cookies because they fit right in the palm of his little hand, and I love them because they don't leave much of a crumb trail behind.

Olive oil
2 bananas
3 tablespoons nut butter (such as almond, cashew, or all-natural peanut butter)
1 cup steel-cut oats
¼ cup raisins
¼ cup crushed almonds

1. Preheat the oven to 350°F. Lightly grease a baking sheet with olive oil.
2. In a medium bowl, mash the bananas together with nut butter using a fork.
3. Add the oats, raisins, and almonds to the mixture.
4. Roll the dough into 16 balls, about 1 tablespoon each.
5. Place the cookies on the prepared baking sheet and bake for 20 minutes, until they are slightly brown.
6. Let the cookies cool for 10 minutes and serve.

Variation tip: Substitute dried cranberries for the raisins for a festive pop of color.

Storage tip: Store the cookies in an airtight container for up to 5 days in the refrigerator.

PER SERVING (1 COOKIE): Calories: 89; Total fat: 4g; Saturated fat: 1g; Trans fat: 0g; Protein: 2g; Total carbohydrate: 13g; Fiber: 2g; Sodium: 1mg; Potassium: 145mg

Nutty Oat Bars

MAKES 6 BARS • PREP TIME: 10 minutes, plus 20 minutes to set **• COOK TIME:** 7 minutes

Steel-cut oats are an excellent fiber source, which helps lower lousy LDL by removing cholesterol from the body. Eating whole grains like oats is also associated with a lower risk of heart disease. Last Halloween, I made these nutty oats bars for a party, using a pumpkin-shaped cookie cutter. They were a delicious and healthy alternative to the bowls of candy—and are welcome any time of year.

Olive oil
1 cup pitted Medjool dates
1 cup steel-cut oats
½ cup nut butter (such as almond, cashew, or all-natural peanut butter)
2 tablespoons maple syrup
½ cup almonds

1. Lightly coat a 4-by-8-inch baking pan with olive oil.
2. In a blender or food processor, process the dates until a paste forms, about 2 minutes.
3. Place the oats in a medium skillet over low heat and toast for 5 minutes or until the edges turn brown. Set aside.
4. In a medium saucepan, combine the nut butter and maple syrup over medium heat, and cook for 1 to 2 minutes, stirring with a wooden spoon.
5. In a medium bowl, mix the date paste, oats, nut butter mixture, and almonds until everything is coated well.
6. Press the oat mixture into the prepared baking pan and place it in the freezer until it sets, about 20 minutes.

7. Once set, cut into six bars and serve.

Variation tip: Add some dried blueberries or dried mango for variety.

Storage tip: Store the bars in an airtight container in the refrigerator for up to 5 days.

PER SERVING (1 BAR): Calories: 379; Total fat: 19g; Saturated fat: 1g; Trans fat: 0g; Protein: 10g; Total carbohydrate: 45g; Fiber: 8g; Sodium: 3mg; Potassium: 489mg

Blueberry Breakfast Muffins

30-MINUTE

MAKES 9 MUFFINS • **PREP TIME:** 10 minutes • **COOK TIME:** 20 minutes

This recipe is a never-fail choice for a quick, heart-healthy breakfast on the way to the mountains or the beach for the day. I enjoy making a batch of these muffins on a Friday night and letting the kids mix in the blueberries. Our last road trip to Nantasket Beach in Massachusetts created lovely memories of us laughing and eating these soft muffins in the car. Not only are they filling and delicious, the fiber helps lower LDL.

Olive oil
2 bananas
1 cup steel-cut oats
1 large egg
1 teaspoon baking powder
½ cup fresh blueberries

1. Preheat the oven to 350°F. Lightly grease 9 cups of a muffin tin with oil.
2. In a medium bowl, mash the bananas with a fork until smooth.
3. Mix in the oats, egg, and baking powder until well combined.
4. Gently fold the blueberries into the mixture.
5. Equally divide the batter into the 9 prepared muffin cups and bake for 20 minutes, or until a toothpick inserted in the center comes out clean.

6. Remove the muffins from the oven and let them cool for 10 minutes before serving.

Variation tip: You can also try chopped apple, peach, raspberries, or pear instead of blueberries in the same amount.

Storage tip: Refrigerate the muffins in an airtight container for up to 5 days or freeze for up to 2 to 3 months. Thaw the muffins in the refrigerator the night before you want to serve them.

PER SERVING (1 MUFFIN): Calories: 112; Total fat: 2g; Saturated fat: 0g; Trans fat: 0g; Protein: 3g; Total carbohydrate: 21g; Fiber: 3g; Sodium: 9mg; Potassium: 238mg

Apple-Cinnamon Quinoa

30-MINUTE

SERVES 1 • **PREP TIME:** 5 minutes • **COOK TIME:** 12 minutes

I love how the scent of fall—cinnamon, apples, and maple syrup—fills my kitchen when I make this recipe. It's the perfect breakfast for a chilly morning. I eat this chewy, warm, and sweet dish while watching the leaves fall outside the windows. Quinoa has a lovely chewy texture, and it is a good source of protein, fiber, and folate. Make sure to thoroughly cook the quinoa because it is hard to chew when underdone.

1¼ cups low-fat milk
1 cup diced apple, divided
½ cup quinoa
1 teaspoon ground cinnamon
1 teaspoon maple syrup

1. In a medium saucepan over medium heat, place the milk, ½ cup of apple, the quinoa, and cinnamon and bring to a boil. Reduce the heat to low, partially cover, and simmer until all the liquid evaporates, about 12 minutes.
2. Transfer the quinoa mixture to a bowl and top with the remaining diced apple and maple syrup. Serve.

Nutrition tip: When increasing fiber in your diet, make sure to do it in small steps, a little at a time, and drink more fluids to help with digestion.

PER SERVING (1 CUP): Calories: 521; Total fat: 8g; Saturated fat: 3g; Trans fat: 0g; Protein: 23g; Total carbohydrate: 91g; Fiber: 10g; Sodium: 141mg; Potassium: 1,078mg

Egg White, Parsley, and Pepper Cups

30-MINUTE

MAKES 12 CUPS • **PREP TIME:** 10 minutes • **COOK TIME:** 20 minutes

Adding parsley is a great way to add extra flavor to recipes while keeping the salt in check. Parsley is available dried, fresh, and even frozen. This herb is also a good source of vitamins A, C, and K, iron, and folate. These colorful cups are wonderful to take on the go and are a real crowd-pleaser for breakfast or brunch potlucks. After a recent party, my friends argued over who would get to take the leftovers home.

1 teaspoon olive oil, plus more to coat the tin
1 diced red bell pepper
2 tablespoons minced fresh parsley
2 tablespoons minced fresh garlic
Sea salt
Freshly ground black pepper
2 cups liquid egg whites

1. Preheat the oven to 350°F. Lightly coat a muffin tin with olive oil.
2. In a medium skillet, heat the olive oil over medium-high heat. Sauté the bell pepper, parsley, garlic, and a pinch of salt and pepper for 3 to 5 minutes, until fragrant.
3. Transfer the bell pepper mixture to a medium bowl and stir in the egg whites and a pinch more salt and pepper.
4. Fill the muffin tins ¾ full of the egg mixture and bake for 20 minutes, until the tops are firm. Serve warm.

Variation tip: These cups are ideal when you need to use leftover vegetables in your refrigerator. Swap out the bell pepper for the same amount of broccoli, tomatoes, or onions.

Storage tip : Store the cups in an airtight container for up to 5 days in the refrigerator.

PER SERVING (1 EGG WHITE CUP): Calories: 30; Total fat: 0g; Saturated fat: 0g; Trans fat: 0g; Protein: 5g; Total carbohydrate: 1g; Fiber: 0g; Sodium: 81mg; Potassium: 96mg

Savory Breakfast Rice Porridge

ONE POT

SERVES 5 • **PREP TIME:** 5 minutes, plus 30 minutes to marinate • **COOK TIME:** 1 hour 5 minutes

This warm and filling dish ups the ante on your typical breakfast porridge, with plant-based proteins and healthy fats. If you prefer, you can swap out the tofu for fish (see the tip) in this savory porridge. I grew up having rice porridge on the weekends when we could sit down as a family and enjoy breakfast together without the rush of school or work.

1 pound firm tofu, drained and sliced into 1-inch cubes
2 tablespoons low-sodium soy sauce
1 tablespoon minced garlic
9 cups water
1 cup rinsed uncooked brown rice
1 cup chopped spinach
Sea salt
Freshly ground black pepper

1. In a medium bowl, place the tofu, soy sauce, and garlic. Let marinate in the refrigerator for 30 minutes.
2. While the tofu is marinating, in a large saucepan, combine the water and brown rice and bring to a boil over high heat, then reduce the heat to medium-high and simmer for 60 minutes, whisking occasionally.
3. Whisk the cooked rice porridge to your desired consistency.
4. Add the tofu and the marinade to the porridge and bring it to a boil, then simmer for 2 to 3 minutes, until fragrant.

5. Stir in the spinach and season with salt and pepper. Serve warm.

Cooking tip: Freezing the rice before cooking it will speed up the cooking process. Place the rice in ½ cup of water, put it in a plastic bag, seal, and freeze for at least 8 hours. The cooking time will be reduced to 20 to 30 minutes.

Substitution tip: If you're feeling adventurous, swap the tofu for a white fish, such as tilapia. Two servings of fish per week is recommended to help with a healthier lifestyle.

PER SERVING (½ CUP): Calories: 276; Total fat: 9g; Saturated fat: 1g; Trans fat: 0g; Protein: 18g; Total carbohydrate: 34g; Fiber: 4g; Sodium: 255mg; Potassium: 377mg

Oven-Baked French Toast

ONE POT

SERVES 4 • PREP TIME: 10 minutes • **COOK TIME:** 30 minutes

Instead of making French toast on the stovetop, enjoy the ease of cooking this classic dish in the oven on a cold winter morning—or any morning. I enjoy this filling breakfast with fresh strawberries and a bit of extra maple syrup drizzled over the top.

Olive oil
8 slices whole wheat bread
3 eggs
1 cup low-fat milk
1 tablespoon maple syrup
1 teaspoon cinnamon

1. Preheat the oven to 350°F. Lightly grease 9-by-5-inch baking pan with olive oil.
2. Cut the bread into ½-inch squares and place them into the baking pan.
3. In a medium bowl, whisk together the eggs, milk, maple syrup, and cinnamon.
4. Pour the egg mixture over the bread, ensuring all the bread is well coated.
5. Bake for 30 minutes. Serve immediately.

Ingredient tip: Mix 1 cup of fresh blueberries with the bread mixture before baking to add a burst of fruit flavor and healthy fiber to this morning treat.

PER SERVING (¾ CUP): Calories: 285; Total fat: 10g; Saturated fat: 2g; Trans fat: 0g; Protein: 15g; Total carbohydrate: 35g; Fiber: 4g; Sodium: 372mg; Potassium: 319mg

Spinach, Mushroom, and Egg White Omelet

30-MINUTE

SERVES 2 • PREP TIME: 10 minutes • **COOK TIME:** 5 minutes

Egg whites are an excellent source of protein and are low in dietary cholesterol and saturated fats. This omelet is a simple, savory breakfast that will help start your day. I love the chewy texture of spinach and mushrooms in my omelets, but you can swap in other vegetables of your choice, such as red bell pepper or zucchini.

2 cups chopped fresh spinach
½ cup diced white mushrooms
2 tablespoons water
1 tablespoon minced garlic
Pinch salt
1 teaspoon olive oil, divided
1½ cups liquid egg whites, divided

1. In a large skillet over medium heat, place the spinach, mushrooms, water, garlic, and salt, and cook for about 2 minutes until fragrant. Transfer the vegetable mixture to a medium bowl.
2. Heat half the olive oil in the skillet. Cook ¾ cup egg whites for about 3 minutes, or until firm.
3. Use a spoon to scoop half of the vegetable mixture onto one side of the omelet and fold it over. Transfer the omelet to a plate and repeat with the remaining olive oil, egg white, and vegetable mixture. Serve immediately.

Storage tip: Store the omelets in an airtight container in the refrigerator for up to 5 days.

PER SERVING (1 OMELET): Calories: 132; Total fat: 3g; Saturated fat: 0g; Trans fat: 0g; Protein: 22g; Total carbohydrate: 4g; Fiber: 1g; Sodium: 405mg; Potassium: 537mg

Tangy Fish and Tofu Soup

Chapter Three

Soups and Stews

Red Lentil Soup
Black Bean Soup
Butternut Squash Soup
Hearty Bean and Quinoa Stew
Tangy Fish and Tofu Soup
Savory Chicken and Watermelon Rind Soup
Chicken and Rice Noodle Soup
Creamy Chicken and Corn Soup
Honey-Garlic Chicken Stew
Easy Turkey Chili
Lean Beef and Barley Soup
Lean Beef Stew

Red Lentil Soup

30-MINUTE, ONE POT

SERVES 5 • **PREP TIME:** 5 minutes • **COOK TIME:** 25 minutes

Lentils are low in saturated fat and a great source of protein, fiber, folate, and iron. They do not require pre-soaking, unlike other types of legumes, but you should give dried lentils a good rinse and pick out any tiny rocks. When I was growing up, lentils were not a common choice on our menu. When I started cooking for myself, it was an adventure to learn about all the different legumes at the grocery store. This soup is an easy, heart-healthy way of integrating more plant-based proteins into your daily diet.

1 tablespoon olive oil
1 cup chopped carrots
1 white onion, chopped
1 cup chopped celery
2 tablespoons minced garlic
Pinch sea salt
Pinch freshly ground black pepper
4 cups water
1 cup whole red lentils, rinsed

1. In a large stockpot, heat the olive oil over high heat. Add the carrots, onion, celery, garlic, salt, and pepper, and sauté for 3 minutes.
2. Add the water and the lentils. Bring the soup to a boil, then lower the heat to medium, and simmer until the lentils are soft, 15 to 20 minutes.
3. Season with more salt and pepper, if desired. Serve immediately.

Cooking tip: Whole red lentils usually take 15 to 20 minutes to cook, but split red lentils only take about 5 to 10 minutes.

Storage tip: Store the soup in an airtight container in the freezer for up to 2 to 3 months.

PER SERVING (¾ CUP): Calories: 189; Total fat: 4g; Saturated fat: 1g; Trans fat: 0g; Protein: 10g; Total carbohydrate: 30g; Fiber: 6g; Sodium: 69mg; Potassium: 437mg

Black Bean Soup

30-MINUTE, ONE POT

SERVES 5 • **PREP TIME:** 5 minutes • **COOK TIME:** 25 minutes

Beans are a staple in any heart-healthy diet, as they help reduce cholesterol, manage diabetes, and aid in weight loss. Black beans are particularly low in saturated fat and contain fiber, protein, folate, and iron. This black bean soup is inspired by a dish that my family and I enjoyed in Mexico. Feel free to top it with some fresh avocado slices for a pop of color and a dose of healthy fat.

1 tablespoon olive oil
1 cup chopped carrots
1 white onion, chopped
1 tablespoon minced garlic
Pinch sea salt
Pinch freshly ground black pepper
4 cups water
2 (19-ounce) cans low-sodium black beans, drained and rinsed
⅓ cup fresh cilantro, chopped

1. In a large stockpot, heat the olive oil over high heat. Add the carrots, onion, garlic, salt, and pepper and cook for 3 minutes until fragrant.
2. Add the water and black beans and bring the soup to a boil. Reduce the heat to medium and simmer until the beans are soft, about 20 minutes.
3. Working in batches, carefully transfer the soup to a blender (or use a handheld immersion blender) and blend until smooth.
4. Top with cilantro and serve immediately.

Variation tip: To give this soup a different flavor profile, add 1 tablespoon of cocoa or chili powder in step 2.

Storage tip: Store the soup in an airtight container in the freezer for up to 2 to 3 months.

PER SERVING (¾ CUP): Calories: 182; Total fat: 3g; Saturated fat: 1g; Trans fat: 0g; Protein: 10g; Total carbohydrate: 30g; Fiber: 10g; Sodium: 51mg; Potassium: 493mg

Butternut Squash Soup

30-MINUTE, ONE POT

SERVES 3 OR 4 • **PREP TIME:** 10 minutes • **COOK TIME:** 20 minutes

This hearty and savory soup has the most delightful color; it is like eating autumn in a bowl! Butternut squash is a good source of vitamin A, vitamin C, and potassium. This inexpensive ingredient is available year-round but is best during the fall. Enjoy a nice bowl of this soup in front of a crackling fire.

1 tablespoon olive oil
½ white onion, diced
1 tablespoon minced garlic
Pinch sea salt
1 medium butternut squash, peeled, seeded, and cut into 1-inch cubes
3 cups water
1 teaspoon honey
¼ teaspoon nutmeg

1. In a large stockpot, heat the olive oil over medium-high heat. Add the onion, garlic, and salt and sauté until the onion turns translucent, about 3 minutes.
2. Add the cubed butternut squash and water and bring the soup to a boil. Reduce the heat to medium and simmer until the butternut squash is tender, about 20 minutes.
3. Stir in the honey and nutmeg.
4. Working in batches, carefully transfer the soup to a blender (or use a handheld immersion blender) and blend until smooth. Serve immediately.

Serving tip: For a spicy kick, sprinkle some cayenne pepper on top before serving.

Storage tip: Store the soup in an airtight container in the freezer for up to 2 to 3 months.

PER SERVING (¾ CUP): Calories: 186; Total fat: 5g; Saturated fat: 1g; Trans fat: 0g; Protein: 3g; Total carbohydrate: 37g; Fiber: 6g; Sodium: 64mg; Potassium: 926mg

Hearty Bean and Quinoa Stew

30-MINUTE, ONE POT

SERVES 4 • **PREP TIME:** 10 minutes • **COOK TIME:** 20 minutes

This stew is packed full of flavor, fiber, and plant-based proteins, making it perfect for lowering cholesterol. The texture of the kidney beans complements the quinoa perfectly in this delicious and filling lunch or supper.

½ tablespoon olive oil
1½ tablespoons minced garlic
1 cup diced carrots
Pinch sea salt
Pinch freshly ground black pepper
3 cups water
½ cup dry quinoa
1 (27-ounce) can no-salt-added diced tomatoes
1 (18-ounce) can no-salt-added red kidney beans, drained and rinsed

1. In a medium pot, heat the olive oil over high heat. Add the garlic, carrots, salt, and pepper and sauté for 3 minutes, until fragrant.
2. To the same pot, add the water, quinoa, tomatoes with their juices, and beans. Increase the heat to high and bring to a boil.
3. Once the mixture comes to a boil, lower the heat to medium and simmer until the quinoa is soft, about 15 minutes. Serve immediately.

Ingredient tip: Garnish this stew with chopped cilantro, fresh lime juice, and diced avocados.

Storage tip: Store the stew in an airtight container in the freezer for up to 3 months.

PER SERVING (¾ CUP): Calories: 248; Total fat: 3g; Saturated fat: 1g; Trans fat: 0g; Protein: 13g; Total carbohydrate: 44g; Fiber: 13g; Sodium: 188mg; Potassium: 908mg

Tangy Fish and Tofu Soup

ONE POT

SERVES 5 • **PREP TIME:** 10 minutes, plus 30 minutes to marinate • **COOK TIME:** 10 minutes

Tofu is a wonderful protein alternative that is cholesterol-free, sodium-free, and low in saturated fat. Tofu is also relatively inexpensive and available in most grocery stores. Soft tofu has a custard-like texture, so make sure to mix it gently when using it in soups. My husband is not the biggest fan of fish, but he enjoys this soup, as the tangy sauce lessens the intensity of the fish flavors.

1 pound white fish (such as tilapia), thinly sliced
⅓ cup Tangy Soy Sauce
8 cups water
4 cups chopped napa cabbage
1 white onion, chopped
12 ounces soft tofu, cubed

1. Place the fish and the Tangy Soy Sauce in a resealable plastic bag. Place the bag in the refrigerator and let the fish marinate for 30 minutes.
2. Once marinated, bring the water to a boil in a large pot over high heat. Add the cabbage and onion and bring to a boil again.
3. Add the tofu, marinated fish, and any remaining marinade to the pot.
4. Bring the soup back to a boil, reduce the heat to medium, and simmer for 5 minutes, until fragrant. Serve immediately.

Storage tip: Store in an airtight container in the refrigerator for up to 5 days.

PER SERVING (¾ CUP): Calories: 181; Total fat: 4g; Saturated fat: 1g; Trans fat: 0g; Protein: 25g; Total carbohydrate: 13g; Fiber: 3g; Sodium: 271mg; Potassium: 541mg

Savory Chicken and Watermelon Rind Soup

ONE POT

SERVES 4 • PREP TIME: 10 minutes **• COOK TIME:** 35 minutes

The watermelon rind usually ends up in the garbage, but not only is it delicious, it also contains many nutrients, such as vitamins A and C. The watermelon rind's texture is similar to a cucumber or a white radish, with a juicy, satisfying crunch. Next time you cut wedges of watermelon for a refreshing snack, cut the pink flesh off the wedges, then carefully slice off the green skin with a sharp knife or vegetable peeler. Discard the skin and use the rind for this delicious soup.

1 tablespoon olive oil
¾ pound boneless, skinless chicken thighs
2 tablespoons minced garlic
1 teaspoon peeled minced fresh ginger
Pinch sea salt
Pinch freshly ground black pepper
6 cups water
3 cups diced watermelon rind

1. In a large stockpot, heat the olive oil over medium heat. Add the chicken, garlic, ginger, salt, and pepper, and sauté until the chicken is no longer pink, about 5 minutes.
2. Add the water to the pot, increase the heat to high, and bring the soup to a boil.
3. Add the watermelon rind once the water comes to a boil.
4. Allow the soup to come to a boil again, reduce the heat to medium, and simmer for 30 minutes.

5. Add more salt, if desired, and enjoy immediately.

Serving tip : Dried scallops are a great topper for this soup.

Storage tip : Store this soup in an airtight container in the refrigerator for up to 5 days.

PER SERVING (¾ CUP): Calories: 157; Total fat: 7g; Saturated fat: 1g; Trans fat: 0g; Protein: 17g; Total carbohydrate: 6g; Fiber: 0g; Sodium: 121mg; Potassium: 290mg

Chicken and Rice Noodle Soup
30-MINUTE
SERVES 4 OR 5 • PREP TIME: 10 minutes • COOK TIME: 20 minutes

I love chicken noodle soup, but restaurant and canned versions are often high in salt. So, I decided to develop my own version that my family could enjoy regularly at home. This tasty, low-fat dish is ideal on cold or damp days. Its tangy flavor, from the addition of the soy sauce, is untraditional but pleasing. Feel free to add some chopped broccoli or bok choy to sneak in a serving of vegetables and add some extra bulk.

5 ounces (150 grams) dry rice noodles
1 tablespoon olive oil
½ white onion, finely chopped
½ pound boneless, skinless chicken breast, thinly sliced
⅓ cup <u>Tangy Soy Sauce</u>
4 cups water
⅓ cup chopped fresh cilantro
Sea salt
Freshly ground black pepper

1. Fill a medium stockpot two-thirds full with water and bring it to a boil over high heat. Submerge the rice noodles in the boiling water for 5 to 10 minutes until soft, or according to package directions, then remove them from the water and set aside.
2. In a large stockpot, heat the olive oil over high heat and sauté the onion until translucent, about 3 minutes.
3. Add the chicken and Tangy Soy Sauce and sauté until the chicken is browned, about 5 minutes.

4. Add the water and bring it to a boil, then reduce the heat to medium, and simmer for 10 minutes.

5. Add the cooked rice noodles to the soup and cook for 3 minutes until fragrant.

6. Remove the soup from the heat. Add the cilantro and season with salt and pepper. Enjoy immediately.

Cooking tip: Make sure to add the cilantro right before serving, as cooking the herb causes it to lose some of its flavor.

PER SERVING (¾ CUP): Calories: 259; Total fat: 5g; Saturated fat: 1g; Trans fat: 0g; Protein: 16g; Total carbohydrate: 36g; Fiber: 1g; Sodium: 335mg; Potassium: 259mg

Creamy Chicken and Corn Soup

30-MINUTE, ONE POT

SERVES 5 • **PREP TIME:** 5 minutes • **COOK TIME:** 10 minutes

This soup has a luscious texture without the use of high-fat cream. The bits of corn and chopped scallion add a nice crunchy texture. I have fond memories of helping my mother make this soup when I was little. Cooking with my mom made this dish tastier, and now I get to share that experience with my own kids.

5¼ cups water, plus 2 tablespoons, divided
3 (14-ounce) cans low-sodium cream-style corn
½ pound skinless, boneless chicken breast, thinly sliced
1 cup liquid egg whites
3 tablespoons diced scallions, both green and white parts
1 teaspoon cornstarch
Sea salt
Freshly ground black pepper

1. In a large stockpot, bring 5¼ cups of water to a boil over high heat.
2. Stir in the corn and return to a boil. Add the chicken and boil for 5 minutes.
3. Add the egg whites and scallions, reduce the heat to medium, and simmer for 5 minutes, until the egg whites turn opaque.
4. In a small bowl, mix the cornstarch with the remaining 2 tablespoons of water, then add it to the soup and stir until the soup thickens, about 1 or 2 minutes.
5. Season with salt and pepper and serve immediately.

Storage tip: Store this soup in an airtight container in the freezer for up to 2 to 3 months.

PER SERVING (¾ CUP): Calories: 254; Total fat: 2g; Saturated fat: 0g; Trans fat: 0g; Protein: 20g; Total carbohydrate: 44g; Fiber: 3g; Sodium: 140mg; Potassium: 560mg

Honey-Garlic Chicken Stew

30-MINUTE, ONE POT

SERVES 5 • PREP TIME: 5 minutes • **COOK TIME:** 25 minutes

Chicken thighs are often overlooked in the grocery store in favor of other poultry cuts, which is a pity because thighs are flavorful, juicy, and inexpensive. Make sure to buy skinless thighs to keep the saturated fat in check. This is an excellent dish for meal prep because it freezes beautifully. Serve it over brown rice for an even heartier meal. I make this stew regularly because it takes less than 30 minutes, and the kids enjoy the salty sweetness of the Honey-Garlic Sauce. I like to serve it right from the pot at the dinner table, so there is even less to clean up.

1 tablespoon olive oil
1 pound boneless, skinless chicken thighs, cut into bite-size pieces
⅓ cup Honey-Garlic Sauce
1 tablespoon white vinegar
1 cup chopped carrots
1 white onion, chopped
1 cup water

1. In a large skillet, heat the olive oil over high heat and add the chicken, Honey-Garlic Sauce, and vinegar and cook for about 5 minutes, or until the chicken is cooked through and no longer pink.
2. Add the carrots and onion and sauté until the onion is translucent, about 2 minutes.
3. Add the water and bring the stew to a boil, reduce the heat to medium, and simmer for 15 minutes until the water mostly evaporates. Serve immediately.

Variation tip: Add 1 cup chopped potatoes to make this stew a more balanced meal.

Storage tip: Store this stew in an airtight container in the freezer for up to 2 to 3 months.

PER SERVING (¾ CUP): Calories: 195; Total fat: 9g; Saturated fat: 1g; Trans fat: 0g; Protein: 19g; Total carbohydrate: 11g; Fiber: 1g; Sodium: 310mg; Potassium: 370mg

Easy Turkey Chili

ONE POT

SERVES 5 • **PREP TIME:** 10 minutes • **COOK TIME:** 40 minutes

This turkey chili is a snap to make and freezes beautifully for extra meals on those busy days during the week. Serve this over brown rice or quinoa for a dose of healthy grains or add your favorite vegetables for even more variety. Don't forget to rinse the canned beans to reduce the salt and make them easier to digest. This recipe is one of my husband's favorite lunches because he can take it out of the freezer in the morning and reheat it quickly for a satisfying midday meal.

1 tablespoon olive oil
1 pound ground turkey
¾ cup Tasty Tomato Sauce
1 chopped white onion
3 cups water
2 cups low-sodium canned tomatoes
1 cup low-sodium canned kidney beans, rinsed and mashed

1. In a large stockpot, heat the olive oil over high heat.
2. Add the ground turkey and cook for about 5 minutes, or until no longer pink.
3. Add the Tasty Tomato Sauce and onion to the turkey and cook until the onion is translucent, 2 to 3 minutes.
4. Add the water, tomatoes with their juices, and kidney beans. Bring it to a boil, then reduce the heat to medium, and simmer for 30 minutes, stirring occasionally. Enjoy immediately.

Leftover tip: After Thanksgiving, use leftover roasted turkey instead of ground turkey in this recipe. Skip step 2, and just heat the cooked turkey with the onion. Add cayenne pepper for some extra spice.

Storage tip: Store the chili in the freezer in an airtight container for up to 2 or 3 months.

PER SERVING (¾ CUP): Calories: 273; Total fat: 11g; Saturated fat: 2g; Trans fat: 0g; Protein: 21g; Total carbohydrate: 25g; Fiber: 4g; Sodium: 72mg; Potassium: 616mg

Lean Beef and Barley Soup

ONE POT

SERVES 5 • **PREP TIME:** 5 minutes • **COOK TIME:** 45 minutes

Barley is a fiber-rich grain with a slightly nutty taste and chewy texture. Different types of barley offer different nutritional values. For example, pot barley is higher in fiber than pearl barley. However, all types of barley are considered good choices for lowering cholesterol. My dad loves to make barley soup in batches for lunches during the week, so we often enjoy a nice warm bowl of barley soup when we drop in to visit.

1 tablespoon olive oil
1 pound lean beef, thinly sliced
Sea salt
Freshly ground black pepper
1 white onion, chopped
1 cup carrots, chopped into bite-size pieces
1 tablespoon minced garlic
4 cups water
¾ cup pot or pearl barley

1. In a large stockpot, heat the olive oil over high heat. Add the beef, season with salt and pepper, and sauté for 3 minutes until browned.
2. Add the onion, carrots, and garlic and cook until the onion is translucent, about 2 minutes.
3. Add the water and the barley, bring the soup to a boil, reduce the heat to medium, and simmer for 40 minutes until it is fragrant, and the beef is tender.
4. Season with salt and pepper as needed. Serve hot.

Cooking tip: Barley will thicken the soup's consistency. For a thinner consistency, add more water.

Storage tip: Store this soup in a sealed container in the freezer for up to 2 to 3 months.

PER SERVING (¾ CUP): Calories: 274; Total fat: 7g; Saturated fat: 2g; Trans fat: 0g; Protein: 23g; Total carbohydrate: 28g; Fiber: 6g; Sodium: 104mg; Potassium: 515mg

Lean Beef Stew

ONE POT

SERVES 4 • PREP TIME: 10 minutes, plus 20 minutes to marinate • **COOK TIME:** 20 minutes

Stews are a comforting family favorite. I remember my parents making delicious beef stews, and as a little kid I would lick my bowl clean to enjoy every last drop. Since having kids of my own, I wanted a simpler, heart-healthy version of that childhood stew for hectic days. I use this recipe to bring back good memories and to make new ones with my own children. Now, I watch my daughter licking her bowl clean after finishing this stew, and it makes me smile.

1 pound lean beef, cubed
½ cup <u>Sweet Salad Dressing</u>
1 tablespoon olive oil
1 cup chopped white onion
2 cups chopped carrots
3 cups, plus 2 tablespoons water, divided
1 tablespoon cornstarch

1. Place the beef and the Sweet Salad Dressing in a medium bowl in the refrigerator and marinate for at least 20 minutes, or up to overnight.
2. When done, remove the beef but reserve the marinade for later.
3. In a large stockpot, heat the olive oil over medium-high heat. Add the beef and slightly brown it for about 2 minutes. Transfer the beef to a plate with a slotted spoon and set aside.

4. Place the onion and carrots in the stockpot and cook until the onion is translucent, about 2 minutes.

5. Add the beef back to the stockpot, with 3 cups of water and the reserved marinade.

6. Bring the stew to a boil and cook until the vegetables are tender, about 15 minutes.

7. In a small bowl, mix the cornstarch and remaining 2 tablespoons of water until smooth and add it to the cooked stew, stirring rapidly until the stew thickens. Enjoy immediately.

Cooking tip: Add some bay leaves to this stew while it's cooking to add a slightly sweeter flavor. Be sure to remove the bay leaves before serving.

Storage tip: Store this stew in an airtight container in the freezer for up to 2 or 3 months.

PER SERVING (¾ CUP): Calories: 272; Total fat: 9g; Saturated fat: 2g; Trans fat: 0g; Protein: 26g; Total carbohydrate: 22g; Fiber: 3g; Sodium: 247mg; Potassium: 791mg

Fish Tacos

Chapter Four
Sandwiches, Rolls, and Wraps

Tofu and Cucumber Spring Rolls
Spicy Chickpea and Cilantro Wrap
Egg White and Avocado Breakfast Wrap
Tuna-Carrot Rice Balls
Seaweed Rice Rolls
Spicy Salmon Avocado Sandwich
Fish Tacos
Lemon-Garlic Tuna Sandwich
Bright Lemon-Cucumber Chicken Rolls
Chicken Pita Wraps with Oregano-Thyme Sauce
Chicken Pesto Baguette
Turkey Sloppy Joes
Lean Beef Lettuce Wraps

Tofu and Cucumber Spring Rolls

30-MINUTE

MAKES 5 ROLLS • **PREP TIME:** 10 minutes • **COOK TIME:** 20 minutes

Rice paper rolls have a fresh, soft, and chewy texture. They are marvelous appetizers to share with friends and family or enjoyed as a stand-alone light meal. Other vegetables to consider adding to these rolls include carrots, red peppers, purple cabbage, green lettuce, or cilantro. I often enjoy these rolls as a side to the <u>Chicken and Rice Noodle Soup</u>, which reminds me of meals from a favorite Vietnamese restaurant.

⅓ **cup** <u>Tangy Soy Sauce</u>
3 tablespoons nut butter (almond, cashew, or all-natural peanut butter)
6 ounces firm tofu, cut into 10 (½-inch wide) strips
5 rehydrated rice paper wraps
1 cucumber, peeled and cut into sticks

1. Preheat the oven to 425°F. Line a baking sheet with parchment paper and set aside.
2. In a small bowl, mix the Tangy Soy Sauce and the nut butter until well blended.
3. Drizzle 2 to 3 tablespoons of the sauce mixture over the tofu strips. You'll have some sauce left over. You can use this for dipping.
4. Place the tofu strips on the prepared baking sheet and bake for 20 minutes.
5. Place the rehydrated rice paper wraps on a flat surface.
6. Once the tofu is done cooking, place two strips of tofu and a few cucumber sticks in the center of one wrap.

7. Fold the sides of the rice paper over the filling, then tightly roll from the bottom up all the way until the wrap is sealed. Repeat with the other wraps.

8. Enjoy the spring rolls with the dipping sauce.

Ingredient tip: Rice paper wraps can be found in Asian markets, in the international aisle in most grocery stores, or online.

PER SERVING (1 ROLL): Calories: 181; Total fat: 8g; Saturated fat: 1g; Trans fat: 0g; Protein: 9g; Total carbohydrate: 20g; Fiber: 2g; Sodium: 255mg; Potassium: 192mg

Spicy Chickpea and Cilantro Wrap

30-MINUTE, NO COOK

SERVES 5 • PREP TIME: 15 minutes

Chickpeas are a good source of protein, unsaturated fat, folate, fiber, and iron. They also have a creamy texture and a nutty taste when cooked. This easy-to-prepare wrap will make chickpeas a new favorite and add some spice to your daily lunches.

2 (15-ounce) cans low-sodium chickpeas, drained and rinsed
½ cup minced fresh cilantro
⅓ cup Spicy Honey Sauce
1 cup low-fat Greek yogurt
5 (6½-inch) whole wheat or whole-grain pitas, cut open at the top

1. In a blender, place the chickpeas, cilantro, and Spicy Honey Sauce and blend until smooth.
2. Scoop ¾ cup of the chickpea mixture and 3 tablespoons of yogurt into each pita. Serve immediately.

Substitution tip: If you do not have canned chickpeas, dried chickpeas can be soaked overnight, then simmered in water for 60 to 90 minutes on low until soft.

Storage tip: Wrap each pita in plastic wrap and store in the refrigerator for up to 2 days.

PER SERVING (1 PITA): Calories: 310; Total fat: 10g; Saturated fat: 1g; Trans fat: 0g; Protein: 12g; Total carbohydrate: 47g; Fiber: 9g; Sodium: 632mg; Potassium: 311mg

Egg White and Avocado Breakfast Wrap
30 MINUTES
SERVES 1 • **PREP TIME:** 10 minutes • **COOK TIME:** 6 minutes

Pre-packaged breakfast wraps tend to be high in sodium and unhealthy fats. That's why I love making this fresh and healthy alternative—and, as a bonus, it comes together in about 15 minutes. My favorite additions to these wraps are red peppers and avocados, but you can choose from a variety of toppings, such as spinach and mushrooms.

2 teaspoons olive oil
½ red pepper, seeded and sliced
½ cup liquid egg whites
¼ avocado, pitted and sliced
2 tablespoons Fresh Lime Salsa
1 (6½-inch) whole wheat tortilla (or pita)

1. In a medium skillet, heat the olive oil over medium-high heat. Add the red pepper and cook for 3 minutes until slightly soft, then remove and set aside.
2. In the same skillet over medium-high heat, scramble the egg whites until cooked through and no longer runny, about 3 minutes, then remove from heat.
3. Spread the scrambled eggs, cooked red peppers, avocado, and Fresh Lime Salsa over the tortilla.
4. Wrap up the tortilla and serve immediately.

Storage tip: Leave out the avocado, and you can freeze these in foil for up to 3 months. Just pop them in a 400°F oven for 30 minutes to reheat for a quick breakfast.

PER SERVING (1 PITA): Calories: 407; Total fat: 21g; Saturated fat: 5g; Trans fat: 0g; Protein: 22g; Total carbohydrate: 37g; Fiber: 12g; Sodium: 488mg; Potassium: 1,099mg

Tuna-Carrot Rice Balls

ONE POT

SERVES 1 • PREP TIME: 25 minutes **• COOK TIME:** 35 minutes

Rice balls, or *onigiri*, are very popular in Japan—with good reason. These tuna and carrot balls are easy to make, simple to pack, and can be eaten on the go without utensils. Bring them for a lovely picnic in the park, enjoy them as a work snack, or pack them for a school lunch. I always feel pampered when I sit down at the park midday and open my lunchbox to see these cute little rice balls.

¼ cup short-grain brown rice, rinsed
¾ cup water, divided
½ cup diced carrots
1 (2½-ounce) can low-sodium tuna packed in water, drained
½ teaspoon sesame oil
Sea salt
Freshly ground black pepper
2 (4-by-5-inch) sheets dried seaweed

1. Combine the rice and ½ cup water in a medium saucepan over high heat and bring to a boil. Cover, reduce the heat to low, and simmer until the liquid is absorbed, about 30 minutes. Remove from the heat, fluff with a fork, and let cool slightly.
2. Place the carrots and the remaining ¼ cup water in a medium skillet over medium heat and cook until the carrots soften, about 3 minutes. Remove the skillet from the heat.
3. Add the tuna, sesame oil, salt, and pepper to the skillet and mix thoroughly.

4. Place the cooked rice in a medium bowl and stir in the tuna mixture.
5. Wet your hands with water and shape the mixture into 2 separate rice balls.
6. Wrap 1 sheet of seaweed around each rice ball and serve.

Cooking tip: It is best to use freshly cooked rice that is slightly warm to the touch when making these rice balls so that the rice sticks together well and the texture remains soft.

Storage tip: Wrap each ball individually in plastic wrap and refrigerate for up to 2 days.

PER SERVING (2 BALLS): Calories: 158; Total fat: 2g; Saturated fat: 0g; Trans fat: 0g; Protein: 10g; Total carbohydrate: 24g; Fiber: 2g; Sodium: 224mg; Potassium: 218mg

Seaweed Rice Rolls

30-MINUTE, NO COOK
SERVES 2 • PREP TIME: 45 minutes

These seaweed rice rolls are similar to *kimbap*, Korean rice rolls made with various fillings. If you're not a fan of tuna, these are also great with lean ground beef, carrots, or eggs. The dried seaweed used for wrapping is a tasty treat that can also be eaten as a snack on its own. My mother-in-law loves to make these soft, chewy rice rolls when we drive up to visit her, and they stave off hunger on the way home.

¾ **cup short-grain brown rice, rinsed**
1½ **cups water**
1 **(4-ounce) can low-sodium tuna packed in water, drained**
½ **tablespoon sesame oil**
Sea salt
Freshly ground black pepper
2 **(7-by-8-inch) sheets dried seaweed**
2 **cups Sesame Spinach**

1. In a medium saucepan over high heat, combine the rice and the water and bring to a boil. Cover, reduce the heat to low, and simmer until the liquid is absorbed, about 30 minutes. Remove from the heat, fluff with a fork, and let cool.
2. In a small bowl, mix the tuna and sesame oil, and season with salt and pepper.
3. Place the seaweed sheets on a flat surface and evenly spread ¾ cup of the rice on one sheet.
4. Place half the tuna mixture and half the Sesame Spinach on the rice along one end of the seaweed.

5. Slowly roll up the seaweed rice wrap, starting at the end with the tuna and spinach, and gently press down to make a firm roll. Make sure to apply firm, even pressure over the entire roll when rolling.

6. Wet the end of the seaweed wrap with water to seal the roll. Repeat to make the other roll.

7. Cut the rolls into equal slices and enjoy immediately.

Storage tip: Wrap the rolls in plastic wrap before slicing and store in the refrigerator for up to 2 days.

PER SERVING (1 ROLL): Calories: 481; Total fat: 14g; Saturated fat: 3g; Trans fat: 0g; Protein: 24g; Total carbohydrate: 68g; Fiber: 7g; Sodium: 498mg; Potassium: 1,312mg

Spicy Salmon Avocado Sandwich

30-MINUTE, NO COOK

SERVES 5 • PREP TIME: 10 minutes

This sandwich is a quick and easy meal to make for lunch or dinner. The avocado provides heart-healthy fats and gives this dish a creamy texture that works very well with the slight spiciness from the sauce. These are my favorite to make for tea parties with friends since they pack such a lovely burst of flavor.

2 (7½-ounce) cans low-sodium, deboned salmon packed in water, drained
⅓ cup Spicy Honey Sauce
3 tablespoons low-fat plain Greek yogurt
5 slices whole wheat or whole-grain toast
1 avocado, thinly sliced

1. In a medium bowl, mix the salmon, Spicy Honey Sauce, and Greek yogurt until well combined.
2. Scoop about 5 tablespoons of the spicy salmon mixture onto each toast slice and top with avocado slices for an open-faced sandwich. Serve immediately.

Substitution tip: If you are not a spice fan, replace the chili powder in the Spicy Honey Sauce with freshly squeezed lime juice.

Storage tip: Wrap each sandwich in plastic wrap and store in the refrigerator for up to 2 days.

PER SERVING (1 OPEN-FACED SANDWICH): Calories: 354; Total fat: 18g; Saturated fat: 2g; Trans fat: 0g; Protein: 25g; Total carbohydrate: 26g; Fiber: 6g; Sodium: 479mg; Potassium: 587mg

Fish Tacos

30-MINUTE

SERVES 5 • PREP TIME: 5 minutes • **COOK TIME:** 20 minutes

These fish tacos are delicious when topped with <u>Fresh Lime Salsa</u> and ideal for both inside or outside on a hot summer day. The low-fat Greek yogurt is a great alternative to mayonnaise, which is high in saturated fats. Greek yogurt is smoother, thicker, and creamier than traditional yogurt. It's also high in protein.

1 pound white fish (such as tilapia), cut into bite-size pieces
1 tablespoon olive oil
Sea salt
Freshly ground black pepper
1 cup low-fat plain Greek yogurt
5 (6½-inch) whole wheat or whole-grain corn tortillas
2½ cups shredded romaine lettuce
2 tablespoons freshly squeezed lime juice

1. Preheat the oven to 375°F. Line a baking sheet with parchment paper.
2. Season the fish with the olive oil, salt, and pepper. Place the fish on the prepared baking sheet and bake for 20 minutes, until slightly golden brown.
3. While the fish is cooking, in a small bowl, combine the yogurt with another pinch of salt and pepper.
4. Once the fish is cooked, place ⅕ of the fish in a tortilla with ½ cup romaine, 1 teaspoon lime juice, and a dollop of yogurt. Repeat with the remaining tortillas and serve immediately.

Variation tip: Add 1 tablespoon of chili powder to the Greek yogurt for a spicy twist.

Storage tip: After step 3, store the components separately in airtight containers in the refrigerator for up to 2 days.

PER SERVING (1 TACO): Calories: 272; Total fat: 7g; Saturated fat: 2g; Trans fat: 0g; Protein: 23g; Total carbohydrate: 29g; Fiber: 2g; Sodium: 450mg; Potassium: 623mg

Lemon-Garlic Tuna Sandwich

30-MINUTE, NO COOK

SERVES 6 • PREP TIME: 15 minutes

Tuna salad sandwiches are a quick and easy way to get the recommended 2 servings of fish each week. This tangy lemon-garlic version of tuna salad is wonderful on crackers, on top of green salads (which lowers the sodium content further), or as a sandwich, such as the one below. Low-sodium canned tuna is something I always keep in the house for meals and snacks.

3 (4-ounce) cans low-sodium tuna packed in water, drained
1 tablespoon Lemon-Garlic Sauce
3 celery stalks, diced
½ cup low-fat plain Greek yogurt
2 (12-inch) whole wheat or whole-grain baguette loaves

1. In a large bowl, combine the tuna, Lemon-Garlic Sauce, and celery until well mixed. Stir in the yogurt.
2. Scoop half of the tuna salad onto each baguette and serve immediately.

Variation tip: Mix in some chopped red onion for color and a little spice.

Storage tip: Wrap the sandwiches in plastic wrap and store in the refrigerator for up to 2 days.

PER SERVING (⅙ SANDWICH): Calories: 353; Total Fat: 7g; Saturated fat: 2g; Trans fat: 0g; Protein: 23g; Total Carbohydrate: 44g; Fiber: 7g; Sodium: 603mg; Potassium: 457mg

Bright Lemon-Cucumber Chicken Rolls

30-MINUTE

MAKES 10 ROLLS • **PREP TIME:** 10 minutes • **COOK TIME:** 20 minutes

These rolls can be eaten without making a mess at home or taken on the go, which makes them perfect for busy schedules. You can serve this type of sandwich roll as finger food at parties. My mother would often use leftover turkey to make similar ready-to-go rolls, and they would always be eaten in a flash.

1 pound boneless, skinless chicken breast
5 cups water
1 cup low-fat plain Greek yogurt
¾ cup diced cucumber
1 tablespoon freshly squeezed lemon juice
Sea salt
Freshly ground black pepper
10 slices whole wheat or whole-grain bread

1. In a large skillet, cover the chicken with the water and poach for 20 minutes over medium-high heat.
2. Remove the chicken from the water, let it cool, and shred it using two forks.
3. In a medium bowl, mix the chicken, yogurt, cucumber, and lemon juice, and season with salt and pepper.
4. Place the bread on a flat surface and use a rolling pin or your hands to flatten it out. Cut the crusts off with a knife.
5. Evenly divide the chicken mixture between the flattened bread slices and roll them up tightly. Enjoy immediately.

Variation tip: Switch it up by adding diced apples for a sweeter version or diced roasted bell peppers for a different savory option.

Storage tip: Wrap the rolls in plastic wrap and store in the refrigerator for up to 2 days.

PER SERVING (1 ROLL): Calories: 143; Total fat: 2g; Saturated fat: 1g; Trans fat: 0g; Protein: 15g; Total carbohydrate: 15g; Fiber: 2g; Sodium: 179mg; Potassium: 268mg

Chicken Pita Wraps with Oregano-Thyme Sauce

ONE POT

SERVES 5 • **PREP TIME:** 5 minutes, plus 30 minutes to marinate • **COOK TIME:** 25 minutes

---

This simple Mediterranean-style wrap was inspired by Greek cuisine. Enjoy it with a Cilantro-Lemon Quinoa Salad or Chili, Garlic, and Onion Kale Chips on the side. My husband loves pita wraps and asks for this one to be put in his weekly rotation of lunches.

---

1 pound skinless, boneless chicken thighs
¼ cup Oregano-Thyme Sauce
1 cucumber
1 cup low-fat plain Greek yogurt
Sea salt
Freshly ground black pepper
5 (6½-inch) whole wheat or whole-grain pitas

1. Place the chicken and Oregano-Thyme Sauce into a large resealable plastic bag and marinate the chicken in the refrigerator for 30 minutes or overnight.
2. Preheat the oven to 425°F. Line a baking sheet with parchment paper.
3. Place the chicken on the prepared baking sheet and bake for 25 minutes until the internal temperature is 165°F.
4. While the chicken is cooking, mince and measure out ½ cup of the cucumber and cut the rest into strips.
5. In a small bowl, mix the minced cucumber and Greek yogurt and season with salt and pepper.

6. Once the chicken is done cooking, cut it into ½-inch strips.

7. Evenly divide the chicken, cucumber strips, and yogurt sauce in the middle of the pitas, fold them over, and serve.

Variation tip: Experiment with the vegetables in this pita! Feel free to add tomatoes, green peppers, and red onions for more color and nutrients.

Storage tip: Store the wraps in an airtight container in the refrigerator for up to 2 days.

PER SERVING (1 PITA): Calories: 258; Total fat: 8g; Saturated fat: 2g; Trans fat: 0g; Protein: 24g; Total carbohydrate: 23g; Fiber: 2g; Sodium: 446mg; Potassium: 495mg

Chicken Pesto Baguette

30-MINUTE

SERVES 6 • **PREP TIME:** 10 minutes • **COOK TIME:** 20 minutes

A baguette is a long French bread with a crispy exterior and chewy interior. This type of bread adds a lovely texture to this bistro-style sandwich. I originally made this recipe with sandwich bread and found that it was soggy, so the heartier baguette solves the problem and takes the meal to the next level.

1 pound boneless, skinless chicken breast
5 cups water
1 cup low-fat plain Greek yogurt
1½ cups Spinach and Walnut Pesto
2½ cups arugula
2 (12-inch) whole wheat or whole-grain baguettes, halved lengthwise

1. In a large skillet, cover the chicken with the water and poach for 20 minutes over medium-high heat.
2. Remove the chicken from the water, let it cool, and finely dice the chicken.
3. In a large bowl, mix the diced chicken, yogurt, and Spinach and Walnut Pesto until combined.
4. Arrange the arugula on the baguettes and evenly divide the chicken salad between them. Slice each baguette into three equal parts. Serve immediately.

Substitution tip: If you are short on time, swap the raw chicken with a low-sodium pre-cooked chicken as a substitute.

Storage tip: Wrap in plastic wrap and store in the refrigerator for up to 2 days.

PER SERVING (⅓ SANDWICH): Calories: 527; Total fat: 33g; Saturated fat: 5g; Trans fat: 0g; Protein: 31g; Total carbohydrate: 26g; Fiber: 5g; Sodium: 499mg; Potassium: 617mg

Turkey Sloppy Joes

30-MINUTE, ONE POT

SERVES 5 • PREP TIME: 5 minutes • **COOK TIME:** 20 minutes

This is the heart-healthy, simple version of a classic sloppy Joe. This recipe takes less than 30 minutes to prepare and is fantastic for a large crowd. It's also great with toppings such as lettuce, tomatoes, red onions, and low-fat cheese. I love my sloppy Joes with fresh slices of avocado because the soft textures seem to melt together deliciously.

1 tablespoon olive oil
½ white onion, diced
1 red bell pepper, diced
1 pound ground turkey
1 cup Tasty Tomato Sauce
5 whole wheat or whole-grain burger buns

1. In a medium skillet over high heat, heat the olive oil and sauté the onion and bell pepper for 3 to 5 minutes. Transfer the vegetables from the pan to a small bowl and set aside.
2. Add the ground turkey to the pan and cook over high heat until there is no pink left, about 5 minutes.
3. Add the vegetables and the Tasty Tomato Sauce to the pan, reduce the heat to medium, and simmer for 10 minutes.
4. Scoop the mixture onto the burger buns and enjoy immediately.

Variation tip: Add a few jalapeño slices in step 3 to give this sandwich some spice.

Storage tip: Wrap the sloppy Joes in plastic wrap and store in the refrigerator for up to 2 days.

PER SERVING (1 SANDWICH): Calories: 380; Total fat: 14g; Saturated fat: 3g; Trans fat: 0g; Protein: 21g; Total carbohydrate: 48g; Fiber: 0g; Sodium: 284mg; Potassium: 467mg

Lean Beef Lettuce Wraps

30-MINUTE, ONE POT

SERVES 5 • PREP TIME: 5 minutes • **COOK TIME:** 15 minutes

Lean ground beef is a heart-healthy, inexpensive protein source that cooks up quickly. Enjoy this meal as a packable lunch or an easy dinner. I love how the crispy fresh lettuce is slightly warmed by the sweet beef inside. If you have some extra cooked brown rice on hand, wrap it up with the beef for a heartier meal.

1 pound lean ground beef
½ white onion, diced
⅓ cup Honey-Garlic Sauce
1 tablespoon white vinegar
10 large lettuce leaves, washed and dried

1. In a large skillet over high heat, cook the ground beef for 10 minutes until browned. Drain the fat.
2. Add the onion, Honey-Garlic Sauce, and vinegar to the pan, and cook an additional 3 to 5 minutes. Evenly divide the beef mixture between the lettuce leaves and fold them over. Enjoy immediately.

Variation tip: Use ground turkey instead of ground beef for less fat.

PER SERVING (1 WRAP): Calories: 172; Total fat: 7g; Saturated fat: 2g; Trans fat: 0g; Protein: 21g; Total carbohydrate: 8g; Fiber: 1g; Sodium: 577mg; Potassium: 99mg

Loaded Veggie-Stuffed Peppers

Chapter Five

Mains

Greek Pizza
Spinach, Walnut, and Black Bean Burgers
Loaded Veggie-Stuffed Peppers
Spicy Trout Sheet Pan Dinner
Maple-Garlic Salmon and Cauliflower Sheet Pan Dinner
Salmon Patties
Sweet Salad Dressing Chicken and Carrot Sheet Pan Dinner
Chicken, Mushroom, and Bell Pepper Skewers
Chicken Curry
Lemon Chicken and Asparagus
Spicy Honey Chicken and Eggplant
Turkey Meatballs
Turkey Quinoa Casserole
Sheet Pan Honey-Soy Beef Broccoli
Heart-Healthy Meatloaf
Easy Lean Beef with Carrots and Potatoes

Greek Pizza

SERVES 5 • PREP TIME: 15 minutes • **COOK TIME:** 25 minutes

This pizza is an easy but impressive dish to whip up for family or friends. It comes together in a snap and feels indulgent, so guests won't complain—even though it's low in fat. Other toppings that are spectacular on this pizza are grilled chicken, red onions, and sweet bell peppers. But go wild and experiment with your own favorites!

1½ cups whole wheat or whole-grain self-rising flour, plus more for dusting
1 cup low-fat plain Greek yogurt
1½ cups Spinach and Walnut Pesto
1 tomato, thinly sliced
½ cup thinly sliced white mushrooms

1. Preheat the oven to 350°F. Line a baking sheet with parchment paper.
2. In a medium bowl, place the flour. Mix in the yogurt ¼ cup at a time until the dough is smooth. Knead it into a ball.
3. Sprinkle 1 or 2 tablespoons of flour onto a cutting board or hard, clean surface, and form the dough ball into a 12-inch circle.
4. Transfer the dough to the baking sheet and spread it evenly with the Spinach and Walnut Pesto.
5. Arrange the tomato and mushrooms on top of the sauce.
6. Bake the pizza for 25 minutes, until the crust is golden brown. Enjoy immediately.

Cooking tip: Make your own self-rising flour by mixing 1½ cups of flour, 2 teaspoons of baking powder, and ¼ teaspoon salt.

PER SERVING (⅕ PIZZA): Calories: 433; Total fat: 31g; Saturated fat: 5g; Trans fat: 0g; Protein: 10g; Total carbohydrate: 33g; Fiber: 5g; Sodium: 279mg; Potassium: 443mg

Spinach, Walnut, and Black Bean Burgers

30-MINUTE

MAKES 6 PATTIES • PREP TIME: 10 minutes • **COOK TIME:** 20 minutes

These tasty, meatless burgers are a great alternative to the typical beef patties. This is also an excellent recipe to have around when vegetarian friends come for a visit. But don't worry, meat-eaters love them, too. Enjoy these patties on a fresh whole wheat bun or with an Apple-Carrot-Kale Salad.

1 tablespoon olive oil
1 white onion, diced
1 cup Spinach and Walnut Pesto
2 (19-ounce) cans low-sodium black beans, drained and rinsed
2 large eggs
½ cup whole wheat or whole-grain bread crumbs

1. Preheat the oven to 375°F. Line a baking sheet with parchment paper.
2. In a medium skillet, heat the olive oil over high heat and sauté the onion until translucent, about 3 minutes.
3. Put the onion, Spinach and Walnut Pesto, beans, eggs, and bread crumbs to a blender or food processor and pulse until combined.
4. Using a ½-cup scoop, form 6 patties and place them on the prepared baking sheet.
5. Bake the patties in the oven for 20 minutes. Enjoy immediately.

Cooking tip: Dry off the black beans with a paper towel before blending to prevent mushy burgers.

Storage tip: Store the burgers in an airtight container in the freezer for up to 3 months.

PER SERVING (1 BURGER): Calories: 383; Total fat: 24g; Saturated fat: 4g; Trans fat: 0g; Protein: 12g; Total carbohydrate: 32g; Fiber: 9g; Sodium: 253mg; Potassium: 461mg

Loaded Veggie-Stuffed Peppers

MAKES 6 PEPPERS • PREP TIME: 15 minutes • **COOK TIME:** 1 hour

Bell peppers are sweet, tasty, and high in vitamins A and C, potassium, and fiber. These tempting stuffed peppers are so tasty that you will forget their high fiber helps lower your cholesterol. Other veggies, such as tomatoes, zucchini, and even acorn squash, also make handy and delicious containers for stuffing.

½ cup brown rice, rinsed
1 cup water
1 (19-ounce) can low-sodium black beans, drained and rinsed
1 (12-ounce) can low-sodium corn, drained
1 cup Fresh Lime Salsa
6 orange bell peppers, halved top to bottom and seeded
Olive oil

1. In a medium saucepan over high heat, combine the rice and water and bring to a boil. Cover, reduce the heat to low, and simmer until the liquid is absorbed, about 30 minutes. Remove from the heat, fluff with a fork, and let cool.

2. Preheat the oven to 375°F. Line a baking sheet with parchment paper.

3. In a medium bowl, combine the rice, black beans, corn, and Fresh Lime Salsa.

4. Lightly brush the outside of the bell pepper halves with oil.

5. Evenly distribute the bean mixture among the bell pepper halves. Place the peppers on the prepared baking sheet and cover them with aluminum foil.

6. Bake the stuffed peppers for 20 minutes, remove the foil, and bake for another 10 minutes until fragrant. Enjoy immediately.

Substitution tip: Substitute cooked quinoa instead of brown rice for a boost of protein.

Storage tip: Store the stuffed peppers in an airtight container in the refrigerator for up to 2 days.

PER SERVING (1 PEPPER): Calories: 279; Total fat: 3g; Saturated fat: 0g; Trans fat: 0g; Protein: 11g; Total carbohydrate: 56g; Fiber: 10g; Sodium: 122mg; Potassium: 1,201mg

Spicy Trout Sheet Pan Dinner

30-MINUTE, ONE POT

SERVES 5 • **PREP TIME:** 5 minutes • **COOK TIME:** 20 minutes

Fish is a good source of protein, vitamin D, iron, and unsaturated fats. Trout, haddock, herring, sole, tilapia, pollock, and salmon are low in mercury and all work great here. These options include fresh, ocean, and farmed fish. I use my favorite—rainbow trout—in this recipe.

3 tablespoons minced garlic, divided
2 tablespoons chili powder, divided
2 tablespoons olive oil, divided
Sea salt
1 pound rainbow trout fillets
2 zucchini, sliced into rounds

1. Preheat the oven to 425°F. Line a baking sheet with parchment paper.
2. In a medium bowl, mix 2 tablespoons of garlic, 1 tablespoon of chili powder, 1 tablespoon of olive oil, and a pinch of salt. Generously coat both sides of the trout fillets with the garlic mixture and place them on one half of the baking sheet.
3. In another medium bowl, mix the remaining garlic, chili powder, olive oil, and another pinch of salt. Add the zucchini to the bowl and stir to combine.
4. Bake the fish for 20 minutes until slightly browned on the edges. Add the zucchini to the empty side of the baking sheet halfway through the cooking time. Enjoy immediately.

Substitution tip: If the chili powder is too spicy for your liking, use lime juice instead.

Storage tip: Store any leftovers in an airtight container in the refrigerator for up to 5 days.

PER SERVING (3 OUNCES OF TROUT AND ½ CUP ZUCCHINI):
Calories: 186; Total fat: 9g; Saturated fat: 2g; Trans fat: 0g; Protein: 20g; Total carbohydrate: 6g; Fiber: 2g; Sodium: 158mg; Potassium: 724mg

Maple-Garlic Salmon and Cauliflower Sheet Pan Dinner

ONE POT

SERVES 5 • PREP TIME: 5 minutes, plus 30 minutes to marinate • **COOK TIME:** 20 minutes

This sweet and savory fish dish is an easy meal to make during busy weeknights. I always keep salmon in the refrigerator or freezer as a staple ingredient, and sometimes get tired of the plain baked version. Adding garlic and maple syrup to the fish elevates it to new flavor heights. The cauliflower provides a sweet and crisp contrast on the side.

1 pound salmon fillet
3 tablespoons minced garlic, divided
2 tablespoons olive oil, divided
2 tablespoons low-sodium soy sauce
Freshly ground black pepper
2½ cups bite-size cauliflower florets
Pinch sea salt
1½ tablespoons maple syrup

1. Place the salmon, 2 tablespoons garlic, 1 tablespoon oil, soy sauce, and pepper in a resealable plastic bag and place the bag in the refrigerator. Let the fish marinate for 30 minutes or overnight.
2. Preheat the oven to 425°F. Line a baking sheet with parchment paper.
3. In a medium bowl, toss the cauliflower with the remaining olive oil, garlic, more pepper, and a pinch of salt, and place it on half of the prepared baking sheet.

4. Place the marinated salmon on the other half of the sheet and bake for 20 minutes until the fish is slightly golden brown on the edges and just cooked through. Transfer the fish from the baking sheet to a plate and loosely cover it with foil to keep it warm. Flip the cauliflower and bake for 10 minutes more, until soft.

5. Drizzle the maple syrup over the salmon and serve with the cauliflower.

Ingredient tip : When buying fresh salmon, look for fillets that appear moist and bright in color, which indicates they are fresh.

Storage tip : Store in an airtight container in the refrigerator for up to 5 days.

PER SERVING (3 OUNCES OF FISH AND ½ CUP CAULIFLOWER):
Calories: 216; Total fat: 11g; Saturated fat: 2g; Trans fat: 0g; Protein: 20g; Total carbohydrate: 9g; Fiber: 1g; Sodium: 293mg; Potassium: 658mg

Salmon Patties

ONE POT

SERVES 5 · PREP TIME: 20 minutes · **COOK TIME:** 40 minutes

This is a wonderful recipe for leftover salmon. These patties help you reach the goal of two fish meals a week and are a stellar source of unsaturated fat and omega-3 fatty acids. I love to serve these salmon patties over an arugula salad for lunch, but feel free to enjoy as a burger, with crackers, or with an extra side of quinoa.

¼ cup quinoa, rinsed
½ cup water
2 (7½-ounce) cans low-sodium deboned salmon, packed in water
1 tablespoon mustard
1 teaspoon Old Bay Seasoning
2 large eggs
Olive oil

1. In a medium saucepan over high heat, combine the quinoa and water and bring to a boil. Reduce the heat to low, and simmer until the liquid is absorbed, about 20 minutes. Remove from the heat, fluff with a fork, and let cool.
2. Preheat the oven to 400°F. Line a baking sheet with parchment paper.
3. In a large bowl, mix the salmon, mustard, and seasoning until well combined.
4. Add the quinoa and eggs and combine well, then shape the mixture into 5 patties.
5. Place the patties on the prepared baking sheet and bake for 20 minutes, until they are slightly brown on the edges. Serve hot.

Substitution tip: Add ¼ cup <u>Fresh Lime Salsa</u> instead of Old Bay Seasoning if you'd like to add some veggies and fresh citrus.

Storage tip: Freeze the patties in a sealed container for up to 2 to 3 months.

PER SERVING (1 PATTY): Calories: 202; Total fat: 10g; Saturated fat: 2g; Trans fat: 0g; Protein: 23g; Total carbohydrate: 6g; Fiber: 1g; Sodium: 480mg; Potassium: 310mg

Sweet Salad Dressing Chicken and Carrot Sheet Pan Dinner

ONE POT

SERVES 5 • PREP TIME: 5 minutes, plus 30 minutes to marinate • **COOK TIME:** 25 minutes

Sheet pan dinners are one of the quickest no-fail choices for meals when you are time-crunched or just don't feel like dealing with a heap of dirty dishes. Since these recipes only use one sheet pan, the preparation and cleanup happen in a flash, without sacrificing health or flavor.

---

1 pound boneless, skinless chicken thighs
½ cup Sweet Salad Dressing
2½ cups carrots cut into thin matchsticks
1½ tablespoons olive oil
1 tablespoon minced garlic
Sea salt
Freshly ground black pepper

1. Place the chicken and Sweet Salad Dressing in a resealable plastic bag and marinate for 30 minutes or overnight in the refrigerator.
2. Preheat the oven to 425°F. Line a baking sheet with parchment.
3. In a medium bowl, toss the carrots with the olive oil and garlic, season with salt and pepper, and set aside.
4. Place the chicken on half of the prepared baking sheet and bake for 25 minutes, or until it reaches an internal temperature of 165°F.

5. After 5 minutes, add the carrots to the other side of the baking sheet and bake them with the chicken for the remaining 20 minutes, flipping the carrots halfway through. Enjoy immediately.

Variation tip: Drizzle 1 tablespoon of honey onto the carrots before you bake them, to match the chicken's sweet flavor.

Storage tip: Store any leftovers in an airtight container in the refrigerator for up to 5 days.

PER SERVING (3 OUNCES OF CHICKEN AND ½ CUP CARROTS):
Calories: 213; Total fat: 8g; Saturated fat: 2g; Trans fat: 0g; Protein: 19g; Total carbohydrate: 17g; Fiber: 2g; Sodium: 298mg; Potassium: 553mg

Chicken, Mushroom, and Bell Pepper Skewers

30-MINUTE, ONE POT

SERVES 4 • **PREP TIME:** 10 minutes • **COOK TIME:** 17 minutes

It takes less than 30 minutes to make these delicious skewers. I love to throw them together on hot summer days to grill outdoors or bring to a last-minute picnic. Oregano and thyme are popular spices in Mediterranean dishes and provide an excellent substitution for salt.

1 pound skinless, boneless chicken breast, cut into 1-inch cubes
⅓ cup Oregano-Thyme Sauce
2 bell peppers, cut into 1-inch chunks
24 whole white mushrooms
1 tablespoon minced garlic
1½ tablespoons olive oil
Sea salt

1. Preheat the oven to 450°F. Line a baking sheet with parchment paper.
2. In a medium bowl, toss the chicken breast with the Oregano-Thyme Sauce.
3. In another medium bowl, toss the peppers and mushrooms with the garlic, olive oil, and a pinch of salt.
4. Thread the chicken, peppers, and mushrooms onto 8 wooden or metal skewers. (If using wooden skewers, be sure to soak them for 30 minutes beforehand.)
5. Place the skewers on the prepared baking sheet and bake for about 17 minutes, until the chicken edges are slightly

brown and it is cooked to an internal temperature of 165°F. Serve immediately.

Cooking tip : Make sure to keep an eye on the chicken. Overbaking can make it dry and stringy.

Storage tip : Store in an airtight container in the refrigerator for up to 5 days.

PER SERVING (2 SKEWERS): Calories: 191; Total fat: 7g; Saturated fat: 1g; Trans fat: 0g; Protein: 24g; Total carbohydrate: 8g; Fiber: 2g; Sodium: 313mg; Potassium: 685mg

Chicken Curry

30-MINUTE

SERVES 5 • **PREP TIME:** 5 minutes • **COOK TIME:** 15 minutes

Curry powder is a spice blend containing ingredients such as coriander, cumin, turmeric, and a variety of other spices. Curry powders are great for vegetables and meats, giving everything a lovely East Indian flavor. This Chicken Curry contains all the exciting flavors without the unhealthy fats.

1 tablespoon olive oil
1 pound boneless, skinless chicken thighs, thinly sliced
1 tablespoon minced garlic
1 white onion, diced
2 tablespoons curry powder
½ cup fat-free plain Greek yogurt
Pinch sea salt

1. In a large skillet over medium heat, heat the olive oil and cook the chicken and garlic until the chicken is cooked through, about 10 minutes.
2. Add the onion and cook until it is translucent, about 5 minutes.
3. Add the curry powder and stir for 1 to 2 minutes until it is fragrant.
4. Remove the skillet from the heat, stir in the yogurt, and season with a pinch of salt. Serve immediately.

Serving tip: Add some chopped cilantro on top to add color and another burst of flavor.

Storage tip: Store any leftovers in a sealed container for up to 5 days in the refrigerator.

PER SERVING (3 OUNCES): Calories: 160; Total fat: 7g; Saturated fat: 1g; Trans fat: 0g; Protein: 20g; Total carbohydrate: 4g; Fiber: 2g; Sodium: 124mg; Potassium: 304mg

Lemon Chicken and Asparagus

ONE POT

SERVES 5 • **PREP TIME:** 10 minutes, plus 30 minutes to marinate • **COOK TIME:** 20 minutes

These golden brown, lemony chicken thighs are a great pairing with the crispy yet tender asparagus spears. My daughter loves anything with a lemony tang, so this dish is a favorite in our home. Luckily, it is a snap to put together after work, especially if you marinate the chicken in advance.

1 pound boneless, skinless chicken thighs, cut into 1-inch pieces
½ cup <u>Lemon-Garlic Sauce</u>
2½ cups (about 1 pound) chopped asparagus
1 tablespoon minced garlic
1½ tablespoons olive oil
Sea salt
Freshly ground black pepper

1. Place the chicken and Lemon-Garlic Sauce in a resealable plastic bag and marinate in the refrigerator for 30 minutes or overnight.
2. In a medium bowl, toss the asparagus with the garlic and olive oil, and season with salt and pepper.
3. In a large skillet over high heat, sauté the chicken until cooked through and browned, about 15 minutes. Transfer the chicken with a slotted spoon to a plate and set aside.
4. Add the asparagus to the skillet and sauté until tender-crisp, about 5 minutes. Enjoy immediately.

Substitution tip: Instead of asparagus, use zucchini as the pairing vegetable.

Storage tip: Store any leftovers in a sealed container in the refrigerator for up to 5 days.

PER SERVING (3 OUNCES OF CHICKEN AND ½ CUP ASPARAGUS):
Calories: 221; Total fat: 13g; Saturated fat: 3g; Trans fat: 0g; Protein: 20g; Total carbohydrate: 6g; Fiber: 2g; Sodium: 352mg; Potassium: 437mg

Spicy Honey Chicken and Eggplant

ONE POT

SERVES 5 • **PREP TIME:** 10 minutes, plus 30 minutes to marinate • **COOK TIME:** 30 minutes

Eggplant can be an acquired taste for some people, but roasting it on a sheet pan caramelizes the edges, producing an absolutely heavenly flavor. And the sticky chili-infused sauce gives the chicken a simple sweet-and-spicy taste that is not overpowering. However, if your guests or family need less heat in the dish, you can easily modify the amount of chili powder in the sauce to tone down the spice level.

1 pound boneless, skinless chicken thighs
⅓ cup Spicy Honey Sauce
2 eggplants, cut into ¼-inch-thick slices
2 tablespoons minced garlic
Sea salt
Freshly ground black pepper

1. Place the chicken and the Spicy Honey Sauce in a resealable plastic bag, and marinate in the refrigerator for 30 minutes or overnight.
2. Preheat the oven to 400°F. Line a baking sheet with parchment paper.
3. Place the eggplant slices on half of the prepared baking sheet, sprinkle them with the garlic, and season them with salt and pepper.
4. Spread out the chicken on the other half of the baking sheet.
5. Cook until the eggplant is caramelized and the chicken reaches an internal temperature of 165°F, about 25 to 30

minutes. Serve immediately.

Storage tip: Store any leftovers in a sealed container in the refrigerator for up to 5 days.

PER SERVING (3 OUNCES OF CHICKEN AND ½ CUP EGGPLANT):
Calories: 248; Total fat: 10g; Saturated fat: 1g; Trans fat: 0g; Protein: 20g;
Total carbohydrate: 21g; Fiber: 8g; Sodium: 370mg; Potassium: 741mg

Turkey Meatballs

30-MINUTE, ONE POT

MAKES ABOUT 20 MEATBALLS • **PREP TIME:** 5 minutes • **COOK TIME:** 15 minutes

---

Whether these meatballs are served atop noodles, alongside rice, or sandwiched in a bun, they are sure to satisfy. They also freeze well for up to 3 months. In fact, one of my favorite ways to enjoy these is to throw the frozen meatballs in a slow cooker in the morning, along with lasagna noodles and some tomato sauce, then come home to the smell of a delicious, ready-to-eat dinner.

---

1 pound lean ground turkey
1½ cups Spinach and Walnut Pesto
½ cup whole-grain bread crumbs
1 large egg
½ white onion, finely diced

1. Preheat the oven to 375°F. Line a baking sheet with parchment paper.
2. In a medium bowl, mix the turkey, Spinach and Walnut Pesto, bread crumbs, egg, and onion until well combined.
3. With your hands, form the mixture into about 20 (1½-inch) meatballs.
4. Place the meatballs on the prepared baking sheet and bake for 15 minutes, or until the internal temperature reaches 165°F. Serve immediately.

Serving tip: Add 4 cups of diced, cooked carrots and celery to these meatballs for an extra serving of vegetables.

Storage tip: Store the meatballs in an airtight container in the refrigerator for up to 5 days or in the freezer for up to 3 months.

PER SERVING (3 MEATBALLS): Calories: 440; Total fat: 37g; Saturated fat: 6g; Trans fat: 0g; Protein: 17g; Total carbohydrate: 10g; Fiber: 2g; Sodium: 373mg; Potassium: 336mg

Turkey Quinoa Casserole
30-MINUTE
SERVES 5 • **PREP TIME:** 10 minutes • **COOK TIME:** 30 minutes

This lovely low-fat casserole will spice up the week and it can be on the table in 30 minutes. The quinoa makes this dish filling and hearty, and the veggies add a pretty pop of color. Make the dish ahead, wrap it in plastic or foil, and freeze it for a future meal—or give it away to friends and family.

1 cup quinoa, rinsed
2 cups water
1 tablespoon olive oil
1 pound lean ground turkey
⅓ cup Spicy Honey Sauce
1 red bell pepper, diced
1 (19-ounce) can low-sodium corn, drained

1. In a medium saucepan over high heat, combine the quinoa and water and bring to a boil. Reduce the heat to low, and simmer until the liquid is absorbed, about 20 minutes. Remove from the heat, fluff with a fork, and let cool.

2. Preheat the oven to 375°F.

3. In a large skillet over medium-high heat, heat the olive oil and cook the ground turkey until browned, about 10 minutes.

4. Add the Spicy Honey Sauce, the cooked quinoa, the bell pepper, and the corn and stir to mix well.

5. Spread the turkey-quinoa mixture in a 9-inch square casserole dish and bake until the top edges are slightly brown, about 10 minutes. Enjoy immediately.

Serving tip: Add some freshly minced cilantro and cubed avocado on top for a burst of freshness.

Storage tip: Freeze this casserole in a sealed container for up to 2 to 3 months.

PER SERVING (1 CUP): Calories: 431; Total fat: 20g; Saturated fat: 3g; Trans fat: 0g; Protein: 24g; Total carbohydrate: 43g; Fiber: 6g; Sodium: 502mg; Potassium: 597mg

Sheet Pan Honey-Soy Beef Broccoli

ONE POT

SERVES 5 • PREP TIME: 10 minutes, plus 30 minutes to marinate • **COOK TIME:** 15 minutes

This is a heart-healthy twist on a family favorite—beef and broccoli stir-fry. This oven-baked recipe creates a crispier beef and broccoli that is just as delicious as the stir-fried version. This is my favorite sheet pan dinner to throw in the oven on a busy weeknight. And choosing lean beef helps keep saturated fat levels in check.

1 pound lean beef, thinly sliced
⅓ cup <u>Honey-Garlic Sauce</u>
2½ cups broccoli florets
1½ tablespoons olive oil
1 tablespoon minced garlic
Pinch sea salt

1. Place the beef and the Honey-Garlic Sauce in a resealable plastic bag, and marinate in the refrigerator for 30 minutes or overnight.
2. Preheat the oven to 450°F. Line a baking sheet with parchment paper.
3. In a medium bowl, toss the broccoli with the olive oil, garlic, and a pinch of salt.
4. Spread the beef on half of the prepared sheet pan and the broccoli on the other half.
5. Bake for 15 minutes until the beef is slightly crisp. Enjoy immediately.

Variation tip: Sprinkle on some red pepper flakes for an extra kick.

Storage tip: Store any leftovers in a sealed container for up to 5 days in the refrigerator.

PER SERVING (3 OUNCE OF BEEF AND ½ CUP BROCCOLI): Calories: 207; Total fat: 10g; Saturated fat: 2g; Trans fat: 0g; Protein: 22g; Total carbohydrate: 7g; Fiber: 1g; Sodium: 265mg; Potassium: 392mg

Heart-Healthy Meatloaf

ONE POT

SERVES 5 • **PREP TIME:** 5 minutes • **COOK TIME:** 55 minutes

Meatloaf is a great dish to put in the oven while you finish up whatever work needs to be done. Try this meatloaf with a side of mashed sweet potatoes or mashed cauliflower. Sometimes I like to add a dash of fresh parsley or Italian seasoning to the ground beef to give this meatloaf an extra pop of flavor.

1 pound lean ground beef
1 cup whole-grain bread crumbs
¾ cup Tasty Tomato Sauce, divided
1 large egg
½ white onion, diced

1. Preheat the oven to 350°F. Line a baking sheet with parchment paper.
2. In a large bowl, combine the beef, bread crumbs, ½ cup Tasty Tomato Sauce, egg, and onion.
3. Shape the ground beef mixture into a loaf and place it on the prepared baking sheet.
4. Spread the remaining Tasty Tomato Sauce on top of the meatloaf and bake for 55 minutes, or until the internal temperature reaches 160°F. Serve immediately.

Cooking tip: Bake four mini versions in muffin tins to cut the cooking time to about 30 minutes.

Storage tip: Store any leftovers in a sealed container in the refrigerator for up to 5 days.

PER SERVING (3 OUNCES): Calories: 269; Total fat: 7g; Saturated fat: 3g; Trans fat: 0g; Protein: 24g; Total carbohydrate: 27g; Fiber: 1g; Sodium: 228mg; Potassium: 463mg

Easy Lean Beef with Carrots and Potatoes

30-MINUTE, ONE POT

SERVES 4 • PREP TIME: 10 minutes • **COOK TIME:** 15 minutes

This is an easy weeknight dinner recipe that includes hearty potatoes and flavorful ground beef that I love to serve with a side of <u>Lemony Green Beans with Almonds</u>. Keeping the skin on the potatoes not only adds heart-healthy fiber, but also gives them an extra-crispy texture.

2 tablespoons olive oil
1 cup diced carrots
1 red onion, diced
2 red potatoes, skins on, diced
1 pound lean ground beef
⅓ cup <u>Oregano-Thyme Sauce</u>

1. In a large skillet over medium heat, heat the olive oil, carrots, onion, and potatoes. Toss with tongs and cook for 5 minutes, until slightly aromatic.
2. Push the mixture to one side of the skillet and add the ground beef to the other side.
3. Pour the Oregano-Thyme Sauce over the top of the beef and toss with tongs.
4. Increase the heat to high and cook the beef, stirring frequently, for 10 minutes, until it's no longer pink.
5. Mix the potato, carrot, and onion mixture with the cooked ground beef and serve.

Storage tip: Store any leftovers in an airtight container in the refrigerator for up to 5 days.

PER SERVING (1 CUP): Calories: 315; Total fat: 13g; Saturated fat: 3g; Trans fat: 0g; Protein: 27g; Total carbohydrate: 24g; Fiber: 3g; Sodium: 349mg; Potassium: 1,025mg

Crunchy Cabbage and Carrot Salad

Chapter Six
Salads, Sides, and Snacks

Balsamic Lentil, Walnut, and Beet Salad
Cilantro-Lemon Quinoa Salad
Avocado and Cilantro Chickpea Salad
Crunchy Cabbage and Carrot Salad
Apple-Carrot-Kale Salad
Corn and Tomato Bean Salad
Tomato Sauce–Simmered Eggplant
Chili, Garlic, and Onion Kale Chips
Sesame Spinach
Sweet Garlic-Vinegar Crushed Cucumber
Lemony Green Beans with Almonds

Balsamic Lentil, Walnut, and Beet Salad

30-MINUTE

SERVES 3 • **PREP TIME:** 5 minutes • **COOK TIME:** 20 minutes

Beets are a good source of folate, potassium, and vitamin C. They add a great burst of color and an earthy flavor to your recipes. If available, add some fresh pomegranate arils to this colorful, nutrient-packed salad for some extra crunch and heart-health protection.

2 beets, peeled and thinly sliced
1 tablespoon olive oil
Sea salt
Freshly ground black pepper
3 cups arugula
½ cup low-sodium canned green lentils, rinsed
¼ cup chopped pecans
2 tablespoons store-bought balsamic vinaigrette

1. Preheat the oven to 400°F. Line a 9-inch baking dish with foil.
2. Place the beets in the prepared baking dish, toss with the olive oil, and season with salt and pepper.
3. Bake the beets until soft, about 20 minutes.
4. While the beets are cooking, in a large bowl, toss together the arugula, lentils, and pecans.
5. Once the beets are roasted, add them to the bowl and drizzle with the balsamic vinaigrette.

Ingredient tip: Leftover cooked beets can be used in shakes or as a simple side dish drizzled with balsamic vinaigrette.

Storage tip: Unpeeled beets can be stored in the refrigerator for up to 2 weeks.

PER SERVING (½ CUP): Calories: 193; Total fat: 13g; Saturated fat: 2g; Trans fat: 0g; Protein: 5g; Total carbohydrate: 15g; Fiber: 5g; Sodium: 198mg; Potassium: 419mg

Cilantro-Lemon Quinoa Salad

30-MINUTE

SERVES 5 • **PREP TIME:** 10 minutes • **COOK TIME:** 20 minutes

Quinoa is prepared like rice—simmered in water—but this grain is protein-packed, full of fiber, and has a pleasant nutty taste and crunchy texture. This tangy lemon-flavored quinoa salad is a great side dish or a stand-alone lunch. This salad is ready in 30 minutes, so why not treat yourself to a homemade quinoa salad regularly?

1 cup quinoa, rinsed
2 cups water
1 cup low-sodium canned chickpeas, drained
1 red bell pepper, diced
¼ cup chopped fresh cilantro
1 tablespoon freshly squeezed lemon juice
Sea salt

1. In a medium saucepan over high heat, combine the quinoa and water and bring to a boil. Reduce the heat to low, and simmer until the liquid is absorbed, about 20 minutes. Remove from the heat, fluff with a fork, and let cool.
2. In a large bowl, combine the cooked quinoa, the chickpeas, bell pepper, cilantro, and lemon juice, and season with salt. Serve.

Ingredient tip: If you find quinoa bitter, rinse it before cooking to decrease the bitterness.

Storage tip: Place the salad in a sealed container in the refrigerator for up to 5 days.

PER SERVING (½ CUP): Calories: 176; Total fat: 3g; Saturated fat: 0g; Trans fat: 0g; Protein: 7g; Total carbohydrate: 30g; Fiber: 5g; Sodium: 97mg; Potassium: 318mg

Avocado and Cilantro Chickpea Salad

30-MINUTE, NO COOK
SERVES 2 • PREP TIME: 15 minutes

This is an excellent summer salad for a "meatless Monday" or as a complement to Heart-Healthy Meatloaf. The combination of avocado, tomatoes, and chickpeas gives this salad a lovely smooth texture. I love to make this for family barbecues.

1 cup low-sodium canned chickpeas, drained and rinsed
1 avocado, cut into ½-inch cubes
2 cups tomatoes, cut into ½-inch chunks
½ cup minced fresh cilantro
1 tablespoon store-bought balsamic vinaigrette

In a medium bowl, combine the chickpeas, avocado, tomatoes, cilantro, and balsamic vinaigrette. Serve.

Variation tip: Add cooked whole wheat pasta to make this salad a more filling and well-balanced meal.

PER SERVING (½ CUP): Calories: 338; Total fat: 19g; Saturated fat: 3g; Trans fat: 0g; Protein: 10g; Total carbohydrate: 37g; Fiber: 16g; Sodium: 248mg; Potassium: 970mg

Crunchy Cabbage and Carrot Salad

30-MINUTE, NO COOK

SERVES 5 • PREP TIME: 15 minutes

When the craving for something crunchy hits, this recipe is my first choice. This colorful, crunchy salad is loaded with vitamins, minerals, and fiber to keep a healthy cholesterol lifestyle on track. My husband loves this dish as a side with most fish recipes.

3 cups shredded purple cabbage
1 cup carrots cut into thin matchsticks
1 cup diced cauliflower
½ cup slivered almonds
⅓ cup Honey-Garlic Sauce

In a medium bowl, combine the cabbage, carrots, cauliflower, almonds, and the Honey-Garlic Sauce. Serve immediately.

Variation tip: Add some cooked quinoa to this salad for a more balanced meal.

Storage tip: Store in a sealed container in the refrigerator for up to 5 days.

PER SERVING (½ CUP): Calories: 135; Total fat: 8g; Saturated fat: 0g; Trans fat: 0g; Protein: 5g; Total carbohydrate: 15g; Fiber: 4g; Sodium: 241mg; Potassium: 379mg

Apple-Carrot-Kale Salad

30-MINUTE, NO COOK

SERVES 5 • PREP TIME: 15 minutes

This is my favorite salad to have on the side with a burger or pizza because the slight sweetness and satisfying crunch balance the rich meat. If you buy a huge bunch of kale, any that's left over can be used in soups, pasta, omelets, or stir-fries. Make sure you take the time to cut out the stem from the kale before cooking because the stem can be quite tough.

5 cups chopped kale
1 shredded Envy apple (or other apple of choice)
½ cup slivered almonds
1 cup shredded carrots
½ cup Lemon-Garlic Sauce

1. In a large bowl, toss the together the kale, apple, almonds, and carrots.
2. Drizzle the Lemon-Garlic Sauce onto the salad and serve immediately.

Variation tip: Massage the Lemon-Garlic Sauce into the kale with your hands to make the kale easier to chew and digest.

Storage tip: Store the salad in a sealed container in the refrigerator for up to 5 days.

PER SERVING (½ CUP): Calories: 153; Total fat: 11g; Saturated fat: 1g; Trans fat: 0g; Protein: 3g; Total carbohydrate: 13g; Fiber: 3g; Sodium: 255mg; Potassium: 294mg

Corn and Tomato Bean Salad

30-MINUTE, NO COOK

SERVES 5 • PREP TIME: 15 minutes

This delicious bean salad can be piled on lettuce leaves, spooned inside a whole wheat pita, or scooped up with baked pita chips. I enjoy this best as a quick lunch when I am looking for a last-minute meal because it is easy to make and easy to pack.

1 (18-ounce) can low-sodium black beans, drained and rinsed
1 (12-ounce) can low-sodium corn, drained
1 cup diced tomato
¼ cup fresh minced cilantro
1 cup Fresh Lime Salsa

In a medium bowl, combine the black beans, corn, tomato, cilantro, and the Fresh Lime Salsa. Enjoy immediately.

Variation tip: Add a few slices of jalapeño pepper for some heat or avocado for a boost of heart-healthy fats.

Storage tip: Store this salad in a sealed container in the refrigerator for up to 5 days.

PER SERVING (½ CUP): Calories: 181; Total fat: 1g; Saturated fat: 0g; Trans fat: 0g; Protein: 9g; Total carbohydrate: 37g; Fiber: 10g; Sodium: 218mg; Potassium: 1,001mg

Tomato Sauce–Simmered Eggplant

30-MINUTE, ONE POT

SERVES 5 • **PREP TIME:** 5 minutes • **COOK TIME:** 20 minutes

Eggplants are a good source of fiber to help lower LDL cholesterol. Instead of using jarred tomato sauce, which tends to be high in sodium, this recipe provides an easy, heart-healthy alternative for pasta nights. This simple but flavorful eggplant dish also goes well as a side dish with the Turkey Meatballs and some brown rice.

1 medium eggplant, cut into 1-inch cubes
¾ cup Tasty Tomato Sauce
1 tablespoon olive oil
2 cups low-sodium canned diced tomatoes
2 bay leaves
½ cup water
1 tablespoon chopped fresh parsley

1. In a large, deep skillet over medium-high heat, cook the eggplant, Tasty Tomato Sauce, and olive oil for 2 minutes, or until the eggplant is soft.
2. Add the tomatoes with their juices, bay leaves, and water to the eggplant mixture and simmer for 15 minutes, until fragrant.
3. Stir in the parsley.
4. Remove the bay leaves and serve immediately.

Ingredient tip: Sprinkle in some cumin and paprika to bring more flavors into this delicious dish.

Storage tip: Store any leftovers in a sealed container in the refrigerator for up to 5 days.

PER SERVING (½ CUP): Calories: 111; Total fat: 3g; Saturated fat: 0g; Trans fat: 0g; Protein: 2g; Total carbohydrate: 21g; Fiber: 4g; Sodium: 45mg; Potassium: 503mg

Chili, Garlic, and Onion Kale Chips

30-MINUTE

SERVES 5 • PREP TIME: 10 minutes **• COOK TIME:** 20 minutes

These kale chips are a fantastic, cholesterol-healthy alternative to snacking on potato chips. Kale is a good source of vitamins A, C, and K, and calcium. When purchasing kale, look for fresh green leaves and avoid yellowing or limp stalks. These crispy, tasty kale chips are a wonderful snack for kids and adults alike.

5 cups kale
1 tablespoon olive oil
1 teaspoon garlic powder
1 teaspoon chili powder
½ teaspoon onion powder

1. Preheat the oven to 300°F. Line two baking sheets with parchment paper.
2. Wash and dry the kale thoroughly.
3. Remove the large stem from the kale leaves, then tear them into chip-size pieces.
4. In a large bowl, toss the kale with the olive oil, garlic powder, chili powder, and onion powder. Use your hands to massage the spiced oil thoroughly into each piece of kale.
5. Evenly distribute the kale in a single layer on the prepared baking sheets. Bake until the kale is crisp and slightly brown, about 20 minutes. Watch the last 5 minutes of cooking carefully as kale burns easily. Enjoy immediately.

Variation tip: Give this snack a cheesy flavor by sprinkling the baked chips with one teaspoon of nutritional yeast.

PER SERVING (½ CUP): Calories: 36; Total fat: 3g; Saturated fat: 0g; Trans fat: 0g; Protein: 1g; Total carbohydrate: 2g; Fiber: 1g; Sodium: 53mg; Potassium: 99mg

Sesame Spinach

30-MINUTE, ONE POT

SERVES 3 • **PREP TIME:** 10 minutes • **COOK TIME:** 2 minutes

This is a version of a popular Korean side dish called *sigeumchi namul*. It is used in various Korean dishes, including *kimbap*, a seaweed-wrapped rice roll (see here). Spinach is a nutrient-packed food for heart health and the fiber aids in lowering cholesterol. This side dish also goes well with the Sheet Pan Honey-Soy Beef Broccoli.

½ **pound spinach leaves**
1 **teaspoon minced garlic**
½ **tablespoon sesame oil**
Sea salt
Freshly ground black pepper
Sesame seeds

1. Place a medium stockpot filled three-quarters full of water over high heat and bring to a boil.
2. Add the spinach and let boil for 1 to 2 minutes until softened.
3. Use a strainer to separate the spinach from the water and let cool. Then use your hands to squeeze out as much liquid from the spinach as possible.
4. Cut the spinach into bite-size pieces and transfer it to a medium bowl.
5. Add the garlic and sesame oil and season with salt and pepper.
6. Sprinkle with sesame seeds and serve immediately.

Variation tip: If you enjoy spice, add some *gochugaru* or Korean red chili powder.

Storage tip: Store the spinach in a sealed container in the refrigerator for up to 5 days.

PER SERVING (½ CUP): Calories: 56; Total fat: 4g; Saturated fat: 1g; Trans fat: 0g; Protein: 3g; Total carbohydrate: 3g; Fiber: 2g; Sodium: 113mg; Potassium: 435mg

Sweet Garlic-Vinegar Crushed Cucumber

30-MINUTE, NO COOK

SERVES 2 • PREP TIME: 15 minutes

This recipe is also called "smashed cucumbers," a popular dish originating in China. It's a great accompaniment for sandwiches or grilled proteins. I often bring it as a side dish to potluck dinners with friends and family. The sweet vinegary flavors really wake up the taste buds, so this recipe enhances the other dishes on the menu.

1 **English cucumber**
1 **tablespoon minced garlic**
1 **tablespoon vinegar**
1 **teaspoon sugar**
1 **teaspoon sesame oil**
Pinch sea salt

1. Place the cucumber in plastic wrap or a resealable plastic bag, put it on a flat surface, and lightly smash it with a hard object, such as a skillet, rolling pin, or mallet.
2. Remove the plastic wrap and slice the crushed cucumber into 1-inch slices.
3. In a medium bowl, mix the cucumber with the garlic, vinegar, sugar, sesame oil, and a pinch of salt. Enjoy immediately.

Variation tip: Add cooked octopus or shrimp for extra flavor and protein.

Storage tip: Store this side dish in a sealed container in the refrigerator for up to 5 days.

PER SERVING (½ CUP): Calories: 58; Total fat: 2g; Saturated fat: 0g; Trans fat: 0g; Protein: 1g; Total carbohydrate: 9g; Fiber: 1g; Sodium: 81mg; Potassium: 238mg

Lemony Green Beans with Almonds

30-MINUTE, ONE POT

SERVES 5 • **PREP TIME:** 10 minutes • **COOK TIME:** 2 minutes

When I was growing up, we always had green beans in our summer garden, and I remember the joy of picking the long, ripe beans from their bushes before meals. These days, I like to vary my green bean recipes by experimenting with different textures and sauces. The crunchy texture of the almonds and carrots perfectly matches the snap of the green beans in this dish.

3 cups water
1 pound green beans, trimmed
1 cup diced carrots
1 red bell pepper, sliced
¼ cup slivered almonds
½ cup <u>Lemon-Garlic Sauce</u>

1. In a medium pot over high heat, bring the water to a boil. Once the water is boiling, add the green beans and cook for 2 minutes, then drain the beans and run under cold water to cool them.
2. In a large bowl, combine the green beans, carrots, bell pepper, almonds, and Lemon-Garlic Sauce. Enjoy.

Ingredient tip: Add a pinch of red pepper flakes to punch up the spice level.

Storage tip: Store in an airtight container in the refrigerator for up to 5 days.

PER SERVING (1 CUP): Calories: 133; Total fat: 8g; Saturated fat: 1g; Trans fat: 0g; Protein: 3g; Total carbohydrate: 14g; Fiber: 4g; Sodium: 254mg; Potassium: 407mg

Chocolate Brownies

Chapter Seven

Desserts

Chocolate Chia Pudding
Cinnamon and Walnut Baked Pears
Peach Oat Bake
Pumpkin Pie Pudding
Chocolate and Date Cupcakes
Blueberry Crumble
Chocolate Brownies
Strawberry-Apple-Lemon Smoothie Pops
Apple-Cinnamon Flatbread
Apple-Honey Cupcakes
Chocolate, Peanut Butter, and Banana Ice Cream

Chocolate Chia Pudding

NO COOK, ONE POT

SERVES 2 • PREP TIME: 5 minutes, plus 4 hours soaking time

Chia seeds are a culinary miracle that can absorb 12 times their weight in water, and they become soft and gelatinlike when soaked. Chia seeds are a good source of unsaturated fat, fiber, protein, and calcium. I enjoy this pudding as a healthy treat . . . or whenever I feel like eating chocolate for breakfast. Instead of low-fat milk, I sometimes use a milk alternative, such as almond milk, for a different flavor.

1 cup low-fat milk
½ cup chia seeds
2 tablespoons cocoa powder
1 tablespoon maple syrup
1 tablespoon vanilla extract

1. In a small bowl, combine the milk, chia seeds, cocoa powder, maple syrup, and vanilla extract.
2. Let the mixture stand for 10 to 15 minutes, stir again, and divide it between 2 Mason jars or lidded containers. Seal and refrigerate for 4 hours or overnight.

Variation tip: Add shaved chocolate, nuts, or fruit (I like raspberries!) on top for a boost of flavor and heart-healthy nutrients.

PER SERVING (½ CUP): Calories: 383; Total fat: 19g; Saturated fat: 3g; Trans fat: 0g; Protein: 14g; Total carbohydrate: 41g; Fiber: 21g; Sodium: 66mg; Potassium: 580mg

Cinnamon and Walnut Baked Pears

30-MINUTE

SERVES 4 • PREP TIME: 5 minutes • **COOK TIME:** 25 minutes

Don't pears seem to ripen on the way home from the grocery store? This is a fabulous recipe to use up any extra-ripe pears you have sitting on the countertop. These baked pears are a lovely fall dessert that fills the house with a decadent warm spice scent as it bakes. I top the pears with a scoop of nut butter or low-fat frozen yogurt for an extra treat.

2 ripe Bosc pears, halved and cored
¼ teaspoon cinnamon
2 tablespoons crushed walnuts
2 teaspoons maple syrup

1. Preheat the oven to 350°F. Line a baking sheet with parchment paper.
2. Place the pear halves on the prepared baking sheet, hollow-side up, and sprinkle with the cinnamon. Fill the hollow with the walnuts.
3. Bake the pears for 25 minutes.
4. Drizzle the pear halves with the maple syrup and enjoy immediately.

Variation tip: Sprinkle some heart-healthy oats on top after baking and enjoy this dish as a balanced breakfast.

PER SERVING (½ PEAR): Calories: 171; Total fat: 3g; Saturated fat: 0g; Trans fat: 0g; Protein: 1g; Total carbohydrate: 34g; Fiber: 6g; Sodium: 3mg; Potassium: 256mg

Peach Oat Bake

ONE POT

SERVES 2 • PREP TIME: 10 minutes • **COOK TIME:** 30 minutes

This Peach Oat Bake is crunchy and nutty—a fiber and unsaturated fats–packed version of a traditional peach crisp. I make this family-friendly oat bake for breakfast, dessert, or a snack with leftover peaches every chance I get.

1 tablespoon olive oil, plus more for greasing the baking dish
2 peaches, cored and sliced
2 teaspoons cinnamon, divided
½ cup steel-cut oats
¼ cup chopped walnuts
2 teaspoons maple syrup

1. Preheat the oven to 350°F. Lightly oil a 7-inch-square baking dish.
2. In a medium bowl, mix the peaches with 1 teaspoon of cinnamon.
3. Scatter the peaches in an even layer on the bottom of the prepared baking dish.
4. In a small bowl, stir together the oats, walnuts, maple syrup, the remaining cinnamon, and 1 tablespoon of olive oil.
5. Distribute the oat mixture evenly over the peaches and bake for 30 minutes until lightly golden. Serve immediately.

Ingredient tip: For a more traditional crisp, swap the peaches for 2 Envy apples, making sure to leave the skins on.

Storage tip: Store this oat bake in a sealed container in the refrigerator for up to 5 days.

PER SERVING (½ CUP): Calories: 394; Total fat: 19g; Saturated fat: 2g; Trans fat: 0g; Protein: 9g; Total carbohydrate: 54g; Fiber: 9g; Sodium: 1mg; Potassium: 742mg

Pumpkin Pie Pudding

ONE POT

SERVES 4 • PREP TIME: 10 minutes, plus 2 hours chilling time • **COOK TIME:** 5 minutes

No need to wait for pumpkins to be in season; enjoy the comforting flavor of this Pumpkin Pie Pudding all year round with canned pumpkin. I developed this recipe so that I could enjoy the flavor of one of my favorite desserts without ruining my healthy lifestyle. Low-fat evaporated milk is a great alternative to using heavy cream in recipes, and the texture is the same.

1 tablespoon gelatin
¼ cup water
1 (12-ounce) can low-fat evaporated milk
½ cup pumpkin puree
1 tablespoon maple syrup
2 teaspoons cinnamon

1. In a small bowl, sprinkle the gelatin over the water and set aside for 10 minutes.
2. In a medium saucepan over medium heat, stir together the evaporated milk, pumpkin puree, maple syrup, and cinnamon. Heat for about 5 minutes, or until it begins to foam.
3. Remove the pumpkin mixture from the heat and stir in the gelatin water.
4. Pour the pumpkin pie pudding through a fine sieve into four small (½-cup) ramekins, cover with plastic wrap, and refrigerate for 2 hours. Serve chilled.

Serving tip: Top the pudding with some crushed walnuts for a nice crunchy texture and some heart-healthy fats.

PER SERVING (½ CUP): Calories: 116; Total fat: 2g; Saturated fat: 1g; Trans fat: 0g; Protein: 7g; Total carbohydrate: 18g; Fiber: 2g; Sodium: 112mg; Potassium: 387mg

Chocolate and Date Cupcakes

30-MINUTE

MAKES 9 CUPCAKES • **PREP TIME:** 10 minutes • **COOK TIME:** 20 minutes

If you are looking for a chocolate cupcake that is indulgent but healthy, this is the perfect recipe for you! Dates are delicious by themselves, so when combined with nut butter and cocoa in this cupcake, the sweetness is ideal. My kids love the smell of these treats as they come out of the oven. We often top the warm cupcakes with a dollop of nut butter.

Olive oil, for greasing the pan
1 cup pitted Medjool dates
½ cup water
1 cup nut butter (such as almond, cashew, or all-natural peanut butter)
¾ cup liquid egg whites
3 tablespoons cocoa
1 teaspoon baking soda

1. Preheat the oven to 350°F. Lightly oil 9 cups in a muffin tin and set aside.
2. In a blender, place the dates and the water and blend until smooth.
3. Add the nut butter, egg whites, cocoa, and baking soda to the blender and pulse until the mixture is a consistent texture.
4. Evenly distribute the batter into the greased cups. Each cup should be three-quarters full.
5. Bake for 20 minutes and serve immediately.

Variation tip: Instead of cocoa, add 1 teaspoon cinnamon and 1 teaspoon vanilla for a more subtle flavor.

Storage tip: Store the cupcakes in a sealed container in the refrigerator for up to 5 days.

PER SERVING (1 CUPCAKE): Calories: 236; Total fat: 16g; Saturated fat: 1g; Trans fat: 0g; Protein: 9g; Total carbohydrate: 19g; Fiber: 5g; Sodium: 176mg; Potassium: 393mg

Blueberry Crumble

30-MINUTE

SERVES 5 · PREP TIME: 10 minutes · **COOK TIME:** 20 minutes

The nutty oat-and-date crumble base is a perfect match for the juicy blueberry ribbon inside this dessert. Its sweetness comes from both the dates and blueberries, which are both rich in soluble fiber that helps lower cholesterol. This blueberry crumble is a perfect afternoon treat with a cup of tea.

3 tablespoons olive oil, plus extra for greasing the baking pan
½ cup chopped walnuts
1 cup pitted Medjool dates
1 cup steel-cut oats
1½ cups blueberries
1½ tablespoons honey

1. Preheat the oven to 350°F. Lightly oil an 8-inch-square baking pan.
2. In a food processor or blender, pulse the walnuts until they are finely ground. Transfer to a medium bowl and set aside.
3. Place the dates in the food processor and pulse until they become a coarse paste. Transfer to the bowl and mix with the walnuts.
4. Add the oats and the olive oil to the bowl and mix until the mixture sticks together.
5. Press half of the oat mixture into the bottom of the prepared baking pan.

6. Spread the blueberries evenly over the oat mixture and drizzle with the honey. Top with the remaining half of the oat mixture.

7. Bake for 20 minutes until the berries are bubbly. Enjoy immediately.

Substitution tip: Substitute other berries, ripe peaches, or Bosc pears for the blueberries.

Storage tip: Store this crumble in a sealed container in the refrigerator for up to 5 days.

PER SERVING (½ CUP): Calories: 375; Total fat: 17g; Saturated fat: 2g; Trans fat: 0g; Protein: 6g; Total carbohydrate: 54g; Fiber: 7g; Sodium: 2mg; Potassium: 387mg

Chocolate Brownies

30-MINUTE, NO COOK

MAKES 6 BROWNIES • **PREP TIME:** 10 minutes, plus 10 minutes to chill

Dates are a wonderful source of fiber and have a lovely natural sweetness. These chocolaty brownies are a great balance between nuts, cocoa, and dates, creating a decadent no-bake, heart-healthy dessert. If you're serving to guests as a party treat, double the recipe and cut the brownies into bite-size servings.

½ **cup chopped walnuts**
1 **cup pitted Medjool dates**
½ **cup nut butter**
¼ **cup unsweetened cocoa powder**
2 **teaspoons vanilla extract**

1. In a food processor or blender, pulse the walnuts until finely ground. Transfer to a medium bowl and set aside.
2. Place the dates in the food processor and pulse until they become a coarse paste. Transfer to the bowl and mix with the walnuts.
3. Add the nut butter, cocoa powder, and vanilla to the walnut-date mixture and stir to combine.
4. Press the mixture firmly into the bottom of a 6-inch square storage container.
5. Place the brownies in the refrigerator and chill for 10 minutes.
6. Cut into 6 squares and enjoy immediately.

Variation tip: Add a handful of chocolate chips for an extra hit of chocolate.

Storage tip: Store in a sealed container in the refrigerator for up to 5 days.

PER SERVING (1 BROWNIE): Calories: 255; Total fat: 18g; Saturated fat: 2g; Trans fat: 0g; Protein: 7g; Total carbohydrate: 21g; Fiber: 5g; Sodium: 3mg; Potassium: 411mg

Strawberry-Apple-Lemon Smoothie Pops

NO COOK

MAKES 7 POPS • **PREP TIME:** 10 minutes, plus 4 hours to chill

Just a bit of lemon goes a long way in these delicious smoothie pops. My kids love being the taste testers before the liquid is poured into the molds. Sometimes we taste so much, the recipe only makes six pops!

2 cups strawberries, stems removed
1 cup unsweetened apple juice
1 tablespoon freshly squeezed lemon juice
1 tablespoon honey
1 teaspoon vanilla extract

1. In a blender, place the strawberries, apple juice, lemon juice, honey, and vanilla extract and blend until smooth.
2. Pour the mixture into 7 Popsicle molds and freeze for 4 hours or overnight. Enjoy!

Variation tip: You can add other fruit for a bit of extra flavor and visual interest, such as raspberries, blueberries, or peaches, when you pour the smoothie into the molds.

Storage tip: Freeze the pops for up to 2 to 3 months.

PER SERVING (1 POP): Calories: 41; Total fat: 0g; Saturated fat: 0g; Trans fat: 0g; Protein: 0g; Total carbohydrate: 10g; Fiber: 1g; Sodium: 2mg; Potassium: 103mg

Apple-Cinnamon Flatbread

30-MINUTE

SERVES 5 • **PREP TIME:** 5 minutes • **COOK TIME:** 25 minutes

This is a fun dessert that can be made alongside the <u>Greek Pizza</u> for a party night with friends and family. Use up some leftover apples for this satisfying cinnamon-scented dessert. I will sometimes add crushed walnuts or blueberries for some texture and color, or a boost of heart-healthy fats, but the original recipe is delicious as is.

Olive oil, for greasing the pan
1½ cups whole wheat or whole-grain self-rising flour
1 cup low-fat plain Greek yogurt
2 Envy apples, peeled, cored, and thinly sliced
2 teaspoons cinnamon
1½ tablespoons maple syrup

1. Preheat the oven to 350°F. Line a baking sheet with parchment paper and lightly grease it with olive oil.
2. In a medium bowl, mix the flour and yogurt together until smooth, then knead the dough into a ball.
3. Lightly flour your work surface, transfer the dough to the floured surface, and press it into a flat 8-inch circle. Transfer the flattened dough to the prepared baking sheet.
4. In a small bowl, mix the apples and cinnamon until well combined.
5. Arrange the apple slices on the dough and bake until the flatbread is slightly brown on the edges, about 25 minutes.
6. Remove the flatbread from the oven and drizzle with the maple syrup. Enjoy immediately.

Cooking tip: Divide the dough into five equal sections to make mini flatbreads.

PER SERVING (1 SLICE): Calories: 213; Total fat: 2g; Saturated fat: 1g; Trans fat: 0g; Protein: 8g; Total carbohydrate: 44g; Fiber: 6g; Sodium: 37mg; Potassium: 340mg

Apple-Honey Cupcakes

30-MINUTE

MAKES 6 CUPCAKES • **PREP TIME:** 10 minutes • **COOK TIME:** 20 minutes

These cupcakes taste like apple pies in miniature cake form. I use Envy apples because I love them, but you can use any apple you like, such as Honeycrisp, Ambrosia, and Royal Gala. For an extra kick of apple flavor, top these cupcakes with applesauce.

½ cup olive oil, plus extra for greasing the muffin tin
½ cup liquid egg whites
¼ cup honey
1 cup self-rising whole wheat or whole-grain flour
1 teaspoon cinnamon
1 cup cubed peeled apple, cut into ½-inch chunks

1. Preheat the oven to 350°F. Lightly grease 6 cups in a muffin tin.
2. In a medium bowl, whisk the egg whites, ½ cup of olive oil, and the honey until well blended. Slowly whisk in the flour and cinnamon.
3. Add the apple to the batter and mix until the apples are equally dispersed.
4. Divide the batter among the greased muffin cups until they are three-quarters full.
5. Bake for 20 minutes, until the cupcake rims are slightly brown. Enjoy immediately.

Ingredient tip: Make your own self-rising flour by mixing 1½ cups flour, 2 teaspoons baking powder, and ¼ teaspoon salt.

Storage tip: Store the cupcakes in a sealed container in the refrigerator for up to 5 days.

PER SERVING (1 CUPCAKE): Calories: 297; Total fat: 18g; Saturated fat: 3g; Trans fat: 0g; Protein: 4g; Total carbohydrate: 30g; Fiber: 1g; Sodium: 283mg; Potassium: 88mg

Chocolate, Peanut Butter, and Banana Ice Cream

NO COOK, ONE POT

SERVES 2 • PREP TIME: 5 minutes, plus 2 hours to freeze

Who doesn't love ice cream? Thankfully, you don't have to give it up when trying to lower your cholesterol. This better-for-you version involves a banana-based "ice cream" that still feels satisfying and indulgent. It's kid-friendly, too! My kids love to be involved in the process of making this healthy dessert, from slicing the bananas to putting everything in the blender.

2 frozen bananas, peeled and sliced
2 tablespoons cocoa powder
1 tablespoon honey
2 tablespoons all-natural peanut butter
1 tablespoon chopped walnuts (or nut of choice)

1. Put the frozen bananas, cocoa powder, honey, and peanut butter into a high-speed blender and blend until smooth.
2. Transfer the ice cream mixture into a resealable container and freeze for 2 hours.
3. Once frozen, scoop the ice cream into two serving bowls and top with walnuts.

Ingredient tip: In autumn, substitute pumpkin puree and cinnamon for the chocolate and peanut butter for a seasonal twist.

Storage tip: Store the ice cream in an airtight container in the freezer for up to 3 months.

PER SERVING (½ CUP): Calories: 269; Total fat: 12g; Saturated fat: 2g; Trans fat: 0g; Protein: 6g; Total carbohydrate: 43g; Fiber: 6g; Sodium: 5mg; Potassium: 669mg

Fresh Lime Salsa

Chapter Eight
Dressings, Sauces, and Staples

Honey-Garlic Sauce
Sweet Salad Dressing
Tasty Tomato Sauce
Spinach and Walnut Pesto
Fresh Lime Salsa
Tangy Soy Sauce
Lemon-Garlic Sauce
Spicy Honey Sauce
Oregano-Thyme Sauce

Honey-Garlic Sauce

30-MINUTE, NO COOK

SERVES 5 • PREP TIME: 5 minutes

You'll want to use this salty-sweet sauce on everything, and it's used in many recipes in this book, so you know I feel the same! Use this sauce as a dressing on salads or as a marinade for chicken or beef. The options are endless.

2 tablespoons low-sodium soy sauce (or 1 tablespoon soy sauce)
1½ tablespoons honey
1 tablespoon minced garlic
2 teaspoons sesame oil
1 teaspoon freshly ground black pepper

In a small bowl, mix the soy sauce, honey, garlic, sesame oil, and pepper together until well blended and use immediately.

Ingredient tip: Buy pre-minced garlic from the grocery store to save time.

Storage tip: Store the sauce in a sealed container in the refrigerator for up to 5 days.

PER SERVING (1 TABLESPOON): Calories: 42; Total fat: 2g; Saturated fat: 0g; Trans fat: 0g; Protein: 1g; Total carbohydrate: 6g; Fiber: 0g; Sodium: 205mg; Potassium: 36mg

Sweet Salad Dressing

30-MINUTE, NO COOK

SERVES 5 • PREP TIME: 5 minutes

Store-bought dressings tend to be loaded with additives, sugar, and sodium—none of which are good for lowering cholesterol. Thankfully, when you make your own dressing, such as this one, you know exactly what's in it. The Worcestershire sauce in this dressing gives it a savory, sweet, and tangy flavor. Use this sauce in beef stews and to baste baked chicken. You can't go wrong when there is a no-fail dressing in your culinary toolbox.

¼ cup low-sodium Worcestershire sauce (or ¼ cup Worcestershire sauce)
2 tablespoons minced garlic
1½ tablespoons honey
2 teaspoons onion powder
½ teaspoon freshly ground black pepper

In a small bowl, mix the Worcestershire sauce, garlic, honey, onion powder, and pepper until well blended. Use immediately.

Substitution tip: If you do not have Worcestershire sauce on hand, you could substitute balsamic vinegar.

Storage tip: Store the dressing in a sealed container in the refrigerator for up to 5 days.

PER SERVING (1½ TABLESPOONS): Calories: 39; Total fat: 0g; Saturated fat: 0g; Trans fat: 0g; Protein: 0g; Total carbohydrate: 10g; Fiber: 0g; Sodium: 136mg; Potassium: 140mg

Tasty Tomato Sauce

30-MINUTE, NO COOK

SERVES 5 • PREP TIME: 5 minutes

Homemade tomato sauce is fantastic in vegetable dishes and meat recipes such as chili and meatloaf. This sauce might remind you of a simple barbecue sauce. If you cannot find low-sodium ketchup, regular ketchup is an acceptable alternative.

---

6 tablespoons low-sodium ketchup
2 tablespoons minced garlic
1½ tablespoons honey
1 tablespoon vinegar
½ teaspoon freshly ground black pepper

In a small bowl, mix the ketchup, garlic, honey, vinegar, and pepper until well blended. Use immediately.

Substitution tip: Low-sodium canned tomato soup may be used as a substitute for ketchup in this recipe. It is lower in sugar.

Storage tip: Store the sauce in a sealed container in the refrigerator for up to 5 days.

PER SERVING (2 TABLESPOONS): Calories: 46; Total fat: 0g; Saturated fat: 0g; Trans fat: 0g; Protein: 0g; Total carbohydrate: 12g; Fiber: 0g; Sodium: 5mg; Potassium: 77mg

Spinach and Walnut Pesto

30-MINUTE, NO COOK

SERVES 5 • PREP TIME: 5 minutes

If you like basil pesto, you will also enjoy this spinach and walnut–flavored recipe. This sauce can be added to sandwiches, meat dishes, bean burgers, and noodle recipes, and can even be used as a tasty pizza sauce.

---

2 cups spinach
½ cup chopped walnuts
½ cup olive oil
2 tablespoons minced garlic
½ teaspoon salt

In a blender, place the spinach, walnuts, olive oil, garlic, and salt and blend until smooth. Use immediately.

Variation tip: Try the same amount of any dark leafy green, or herbs such as kale, chard, parsley, or basil, in place of the spinach.

Storage tip: Store the sauce in a sealed container in the refrigerator for up to 5 days, or freeze the sauce in ice cube trays and cover for up to 1 month.

PER SERVING (¼ CUP): Calories: 275; Total fat: 29g; Saturated fat: 4g; Trans fat: 0g; Protein: 2g; Total carbohydrate: 3g; Fiber: 1g; Sodium: 243mg; Potassium: 132mg

Fresh Lime Salsa

30-MINUTE, NO COOK

SERVES 5 • PREP TIME: 10 minutes

Salsa is a versatile condiment that is great as a dip or as a tasty addition to bean and fish dishes. Surround this salsa with cut vegetables, tortilla chips, or toasted flatbread at your next picnic or gathering. If you are feeling adventurous, substitute fresh chopped apples or mangoes for the lime juice.

---

3 tomatoes, coarsely chopped
¼ cup chopped white onion
¼ cup chopped fresh cilantro
1 tablespoon minced garlic
1 tablespoon freshly squeezed lime juice
Sea salt

In a blender, place the tomatoes, onion, cilantro, garlic, and lime juice and blend until smooth. Season with salt and use immediately.

Variation tip: Add some chopped jalapeño peppers to kick up the heat.

Storage tip: Store the salsa in a sealed container in the refrigerator for up to 5 days.

PER SERVING (3 TABLESPOONS): Calories: 20; Total fat: 0g; Saturated fat: 0g; Trans fat: 0g; Protein: 1g; Total carbohydrate: 4g; Fiber: 1g; Sodium: 36mg; Potassium: 201mg

Tangy Soy Sauce

30-MINUTE, NO COOK

SERVES 5 • PREP TIME: 5 minutes

Store-bought soy and fish sauces are very high in sodium, so creating a healthier, heart-friendly alternative was at the top of my list. This sauce perks up soup and gives a delicious flavor to tofu, chicken, or fish. It can also make fishy dishes taste less pungent for people who are not the biggest fans of fish.

2 tablespoons low-sodium soy sauce (or 1 tablespoon soy sauce)
1½ tablespoons honey
1 tablespoon white vinegar
1 tablespoon minced garlic
1 teaspoon peeled minced fresh ginger

In a small bowl, mix the soy sauce, honey, vinegar, garlic, and ginger until well blended. Use immediately.

Substitution tip: Feel free to swap in rice vinegar if you have any in the pantry. It is generally sweeter than white vinegar, which has a strong, sour flavor.

Storage tip: Store the sauce in a sealed container in the refrigerator for up to 5 days.

PER SERVING (1 TABLESPOON): Calories: 26; Total fat: 0g; Saturated fat: 0g; Trans fat: 0g; Protein: 1g; Total carbohydrate: 6g; Fiber: 0g; Sodium: 205mg; Potassium: 32mg

Lemon-Garlic Sauce

30-MINUTE, NO COOK

SERVES 5 • PREP TIME: 5 minutes

This lovely sauce works wonders both as a salad dressing and as a chicken marinade. It is my daughter's favorite since she loves all things lemon. You can create complexity in the flavor by using an assortment of citrus juices such as lime, orange, and lemon.

¼ **cup freshly squeezed lemon juice**
2 **tablespoons olive oil**
1 **tablespoon minced garlic**
1 **tablespoon dried oregano**
½ **teaspoon salt**

In a small bowl, mix the lemon juice, olive oil, garlic, oregano, and salt until well blended. Use immediately.

Leftover tip: Freeze leftover fresh lemon juice in ice cube trays for use in another recipe.

Storage tip: Store the sauce in a sealed container in the refrigerator for up to 5 days.

PER SERVING (1½ TABLESPOONS): Calories: 55; Total fat: 5g; Saturated fat: 1g; Trans fat: 0g; Protein: 0g; Total carbohydrate: 2g; Fiber: 0g; Sodium: 233mg; Potassium: 27mg

Spicy Honey Sauce

30-MINUTE, NO COOK

SERVES 5 • PREP TIME: 5 minutes

Look no further than this sauce to add a nice heat to chickpeas, fish, and poultry dishes. If you enjoy the sweet garlicky flavor but find the chili powder too spicy, then use fresh lime juice instead.

---

2 tablespoons vegetable oil
1½ tablespoons honey
1 tablespoon minced garlic
1 tablespoon chili powder
½ teaspoon salt

In a small bowl, mix the vegetable oil, honey, garlic, chili powder, and salt until well blended. Use immediately.

Serving tip: Heat the sauce briefly in the microwave and serve as a dipping sauce for the Seaweed Rice Rolls.

Storage tip: Store the sauce in a sealed container in the refrigerator for up to 5 days.

PER SERVING (1 TABLESPOON): Calories: 78; Total fat: 6g; Saturated fat: 0g; Trans fat: 0g; Protein: 0g; Total carbohydrate: 7g; Fiber: 1g; Sodium: 279mg; Potassium: 41mg

Oregano-Thyme Sauce

30-MINUTE, NO COOK

SERVES 5 • PREP TIME: 5 minutes

This sauce can be used in many ways other than as a salad dressing. Why not try it as a savory marinade for meat or poultry? Use fresh minced oregano and thyme from your summer garden or window boxes for an incredibly intense herbal flavor.

2 tablespoons balsamic vinegar
1 tablespoon dried oregano
1 tablespoon dried thyme
1 tablespoon minced garlic
½ teaspoon salt

In a small bowl, mix the vinegar, oregano, thyme, garlic, and salt until well blended. Use immediately.

Ingredient tip: A good-quality balsamic vinegar will be thick and sweet, and choosing the best one is similar to picking wine. Cheaper vinegars may not have the same depth of flavors, so go with at least a mid-priced product.

Storage tip: Store the sauce in a sealed container in the refrigerator for up to 5 days.

PER SERVING (1 TABLESPOON): Calories: 10; Total fat: 0g; Saturated fat: 0g; Trans fat: 0g; Protein: 0g; Total carbohydrate: 2g; Fiber: 0g; Sodium: 235mg; Potassium: 25mg

Measurement Conversions

VOLUME EQUIVALENTS	U.S. STANDARD	U.S. STANDARD (OUNCES)	METRIC (APPROXIMATE)
LIQUID	2 tablespoons	1 fl. oz.	30 mL
	¼ cup	2 fl. oz.	60 mL
	½ cup	4 fl. oz.	120 mL
	1 cup	8 fl. oz.	240 mL
	1½ cups	12 fl. oz.	355 mL
	2 cups or 1 pint	16 fl. oz.	475 mL
	4 cups or 1 quart	32 fl. oz.	1 L
	1 gallon	128 fl. oz.	4 L
DRY	⅛ teaspoon	—	0.5 mL
	¼ teaspoon	—	1 mL
	½ teaspoon	—	2 mL
	¾ teaspoon	—	4 mL
	1 teaspoon	—	5 mL
	1 tablespoon	—	15 mL
	¼ cup	—	59 mL
	⅓ cup	—	79 mL
	½ cup	—	118 mL
	⅔ cup	—	156 mL
	¾ cup	—	177 mL
	1 cup	—	235 mL
	2 cups or 1 pint	—	475 mL
	3 cups	—	700 mL
	4 cups or 1 quart	—	1 L
	½ gallon	—	2 L
	1 gallon	—	4 L

OVEN TEMPERATURES

FAHRENHEIT	CELSIUS (APPROXIMATE)
250°F	120°C
300°F	150°C
325°F	165°C
350°F	180°C
375°F	190°C
400°F	200°C
425°F	220°C
450°F	230°C

WEIGHT EQUIVALENTS

U.S. STANDARD	METRIC (APPROXIMATE)
½ ounce	15 g
1 ounce	30 g
2 ounces	60 g
4 ounces	115 g
8 ounces	225 g
12 ounces	340 g
16 ounces or 1 pound	455 g

Resources

Academy of Nutrition and Dietetics: the American source for science-based food and nutrition information. EatRight.org

American Heart Association: an American voluntary association dedicated to fighting heart disease and stroke. Heart.org

Dietitians of Canada: the Canadian source of expertise in areas of food, nutrition, and health. Dietitians.ca

Heart & Stroke: A Canadian voluntary association dedicated to fighting heart disease and stroke. HeartAndStroke.ca

References

Academy of Nutrition and Dietetics. The Basics of the nutrition facts label. Accessed February 2020. EatRight.org/food/nutrition/nutrition-facts-and-food-labels/the-basics-of-the-nutrition-facts-label

American Heart Association. "Control Your Cholesterol." April 30, 2017. Heart.org/en/health-topics/cholesterol/about-cholesterol

American Heart Association. "Emergency signs: When to call 911." 2020. HeartAndStroke.ca/heart/emergency-signs/heart-attack-and-stroke

American Heart Association. "Food Packaging Claims." March 6, 2017. Heart.org/en/healthy-living/healthy-eating/eat-smart/nutrition-basics/food-packaging-claims

American Heart Association. "HDL (good), LDL (bad) Cholesterol and Triglycerides." April 30, 2017. Heart.org/en/health-topics/cholesterol/hdl-good-ldl-bad-cholesterol-and-triglycerides

American Heart Association. "High Blood Pressure." 2020. HeartAndStroke.ca/heart/risk-and-prevention/condition-risk-factors/high-blood-pressure?gclid=EAIaIQobChMIv5bruPzA6QIVAz6tBh2_bwaqEAAYASAAEgLYDvD_BwE&gclsrc=aw.ds

American Heart Association. "Saturated Fat." 2020. Heart.org/en/healthy-living/healthy-eating/eat-smart/fats/saturated-fats

American Heart Association. "Understanding ingredients on food labels." March 6, 2017. Heart.org/en/healthy-living/healthy-eating/eat-smart/nutrition-basics/understanding-ingredients-on-food-labels

American Heart Association. "Whole Grains. Refined Grains. Dietary Fiber." September 20, 2016. Heart.org/en/healthy-living/healthy-eating/eat-smart/nutrition-basics/whole-grains-refined-grains-and-dietary-fiber

Arnett, Donna K., Roger S. Blumenthal, Michelle A. Albert, Andrew B. Buroker, Zachary D. Goldberger, Ellen J. Hahn, Cheryl Dennison Himmelfarb, et al. 2019 ACC/AHA "Guideline on the Primary Prevention of Cardiovascular Disease: Executive Summary: A Report of the American College of Cardiology/American Heart Association Task Force on Clinical Practice Guidelines." *Circulation*. 2019; 140: e563-e595. DOI.org/10.1161/CIR.0000000000000677

ATP III Final Report. V. AHA Journals. "Adopting Healthful Lifestyle Habits to Lower LDL Cholesterol and Reduce CHD Risk." *Circulation*. 2002;106:3253–3280. DOI.org/10.1161/circ.106.25.3253

Carson, Jo Ann S., Alice H. Lichtenstein, Cheryl A.M. Anderson, Lawrence J. Appel, Penny M. Kris-Etherton, Katie A. Meyer, Kristina Petersen, et al. "Dietary Cholesterol and Cardiovascular Risk: A Science Advisory From the American Heart Association." *Circulation*. 2020;141:e39–e53. DOI.org/10.1161/CIR.0000000000000743

Centers for Disease Control and Prevention. "Cholesterol: Knowing your risk." January 31, 2020. CDC.gov/cholesterol/risk_factors.htm

Cleveland Clinic. "Fat: What you need to know." November 28, 2014. my.ClevelandClinic.org/health/articles/11208-fat-what-you-need-to-know

Dietitians of Canada. "All About Barley." Nov 28, 2017. UnlockFood.ca/en/Articles/Cooking-And-Food/Grain-Products/All-About-Barley.aspx

Dietitians of Canada. "All About Beans." March 21, 2019. UnlockFood.ca/en/Articles/Budget/All-About-Beans.aspx

Dietitians of Canada. "All About Evaporated Milk." June 10, 2020. UnlockFood.ca/en/Articles/Cooking-And-Food/Milk,-Yogurt-and-Cheese/All-About-Evaporated-Milk.aspx

Dietitians of Canada. "All About Fall Harvest Vegetables." November 28, 2017. UnlockFood.ca/en/Articles/Cooking-Food-Preparation/Fall-Harvest-Vegetables.aspx (Article removed)

Dietitians of Canada. "All About Fish." February 27, 2019. UnlockFood.ca/en/Articles/Cooking-And-Food/Meat,-Poultry,-Eggs-and-Fish/All-About-Fish.aspx (Article removed)

Dietitians of Canada. "All About Kale." October 4, 2017. UnlockFood.ca/en/Articles/Cooking-And-Food/Vegetables-and-Fruit/All-About-Kale.aspx (Article removed)

Dietitians of Canada. "All About Oats."(January 29, 2019). UnlockFood.ca/en/Articles/Heart-Health/All-About-Oats.aspx

Dietitians of Canada. "All About Quinoa." March 10, 2017. UnlockFood.ca/en/Articles/Cooking-And-Food/Grain-Products/All-About-Quinoa.aspx

Dietitians of Canada. "All About Tofu." September 19, 2017. UnlockFood.ca/en/Articles/Cooking-Food-Preparation/Everything-You-Need-to-Know-About-Tofu!.aspx

Harvard Health Publishing. "How to choose healthy yogurt." August 2013. health.Harvard.edu/staying-healthy/how-to-choose-a-healthy-yogurt

Harvard T.H. Chan School of Public Health. "The Nutrition Source: Banana." 2020. HSPH.Harvard.edu/nutritionsource/food-features/bananas

Harvard T.H. Chan School of Public Health. "The Nutrition Source: Chickpeas." 2020. HSPH.Harvard.edu/nutritionsource/food-features/chickpeas-garbanzo-beans

Harvard T.H. Chan School of Public Health. "The Nutrition Source: Cholesterol." 2020. HSPH.Harvard.edu/nutritionsource/what-should-you-eat/fats-and-cholesterol/cholesterol

Harvard T.H. Chan School of Public Health. "The Nutrition Source: Lentils." 2020. HSPH.Harvard.edu/nutritionsource/food-features/lentils

Heart and Stroke Foundation of Canada. "Managing Cholesterol." 2020. HeartAndStroke.ca/heart/risk-and-prevention/condition-risk-factors/managing-cholesterol

USA Food and Drug Administration. "How to Understand and Use Nutrition Facts Label." March 11, 2020. FDA.gov/food/new-nutrition-facts-label/how-understand-and-use-nutrition-facts-label

Van Horn, Linda, Jo Ann S. Carson, Lawrence J. Appel, Lora E. Burke, Christina Economos, Wahida Karmally, Kristie Lancaster, et al. "Recommended Dietary Pattern to Achieve Adherence to the American Heart Association/ American College of Cardiology (AHA/ACC) Guidelines: A Scientific Statement from the American Heart Association." *Circulation*. 2016; 134: e505-e529. DOI: 10.1161/CIR.0000000000000469

Wadhera, Rishi K., Dylan L. Steen, Irfan Khan, Robert P. Giugliano, and JoAnne M. Foody. "A review of low-density lipoprotein cholesterol, treatment strategies, and its impact on cardiovascular disease morbidity and mortality." *Journal of Clinical Lipidology*. 2016; 10, 472-489. DOI.org/10.1016/j.jacl.2015.11.010

198

Printed in Great Britain
by Amazon

40057472R10119